Communication in the Public Interest

Communication has never been more important than in our current cultural moment. From the growing monopolization of global media, to human rights issues, health campaigns, and issues of free speech and society, communication has real political and ethical consequences. The books in this ICA Wiley-Blackwell *Communication in the Public Interest* series are accessible and definitive treatments of subjects central to understanding communication and its intersections to the wider world; they will widen understanding, encourage discussion, and illuminate the importance of communicating about issues that affect people's lives.

Already published

Susan Moeller: *Packaging Terrorism: Co-opting the News for Politics and Profit*
Roxanne Parrott: *Talking about Health: Why Communication Matters*

Forthcoming

Nadia Caidi: *Right to Know: Information Post 9/11*
Karen Ross and Stephen Coleman: *Them and Us: The Media and the Public*
Michael Delli Carpini: *Beyond the Ivory Tower: Communication and the Public Interest*

Talking about Health

Why Communication Matters

Roxanne Parrott

WILEY-BLACKWELL

A John Wiley & Sons, Ltd., Publication

This edition first published 2009
© 2009 Roxanne Parrott

Blackwell Publishing was acquired by John Wiley & Sons in February 2007. Blackwell's publishing program has been merged with Wiley's global Scientific, Technical, and Medical business to form Wiley-Blackwell.

Registered Office
John Wiley & Sons Ltd, The Atrium, Southern Gate, Chichester, West Sussex, PO19 8SQ, United Kingdom

Editorial Offices
350 Main Street, Malden, MA 02148-5020, USA
9600 Garsington Road, Oxford, OX4 2DQ, UK
The Atrium, Southern Gate, Chichester, West Sussex, PO19 8SQ, UK

For details of our global editorial offices, for customer services, and for information about how to apply for permission to reuse the copyright material in this book please see our website at www.wiley.com/wiley-blackwell.

The right of Roxanne Parrott to be identified as the author of this work has been asserted in accordance with the Copyright, Designs and Patents Act 1988.

Wiley also publishes its books in a variety of electronic formats. Some content that appears in print may not be available in electronic books.

Designations used by companies to distinguish their products are often claimed as trademarks. All brand names and product names used in this book are trade names, service marks, trademarks or registered trademarks of their respective owners. The publisher is not associated with any product or vendor mentioned in this book. This publication is designed to provide accurate and authoritative information in regard to the subject matter covered. It is sold on the understanding that the publisher is not engaged in rendering professional services. If professional advice or other expert assistance is required, the services of a competent professional should be sought.

Library of Congress Cataloging-in-Publication Data

Parrott, Roxanne.
  Talking about health : why communication matters / Roxanne Parrott.
    p. cm. — (Communication in the public interest)
  Includes bibliographical references and index.
  ISBN 978-1-4051-7757-3 (hardcover : alk. paper) — ISBN 978-1-4051-7756-6 (pbk. : alk. paper)   1. Communication in medicine.   2. Interpersonal communication.   I. Title.
  R118.P376 2009
  610.69′9—dc22

                                                                    2008055180

A catalogue record for this book is available from the British Library.

Set in 10.5 pt Photina by Graphicraft Limited, Hong Kong
Printed in Singapore by Ho Printing Singapore Pte Ltd

01   2009

For my Dad, Niley Allan Louiselle,
with love and thanks for his advice:
"If it's important to you, do it . . ."
And so I have done many things I wouldn't have
otherwise done
including writing this book.

Contents

Contents
ix

Preface

No one ever says when lying on their death bed, "I sure wish I'd worked harder. I needed to put in more hours at the office. I could've spent weekends working and met more deadlines, finished more on my 'to-do' list, and gotten more rewards for working hard." But people often do say, "I wish I'd paid more attention to my health, so I could have more time with my family and see more places I always wanted to see." Or, as my husband's grandmother confided to me, "I wish I'd eaten more ice cream and less beans." With so much knowledge about health and so many ways to aid our health, why would any of us be wishing we'd paid more attention to our health? That's a loaded question. And there are many answers. One fundamental one has to do with communication. And that's why I've written this book.

There are *better* versus *worse* ways to talk about health. Because we don't often think much about why communication about health matters, we don't talk about health in our families or with our friends in ways that help us make better choices. We're challenged to make sense of conversations with families and friends that conflict with advice from our doctors, what we've heard on TV, seen in the movies, or read in a magazine or chat room on the internet. We're challenged by media images that look like no one we know and movies where the main characters work all day and play all night, eat and drink to excess but don't have heart disease and don't die from colon cancer. There are patterns in the talk and images, however, that we can look for and, knowing that they are there, make better decisions. Sometimes, profit is the primary motive in talk about health. Sometimes, entertainment is *just* entertainment.

In this book, I'm opening my "family album" to put a lens over talk about health. I do this, not because my family is unusual but because it's just like everyone else's. I'm hopeful that by sharing my family's experiences, every reader will see themselves and their families in the talk, and it will improve their conversations about health and sometimes health itself. My view of communicating about health is situated within these experiences. I am a daughter who received health care in the military system for the first two decades of her life, a wife who received maternity care through the employment of her spouse at IBM, and now a faculty member with benefits through the university settings where I teach and conduct research. My major as an undergraduate included political science and my minor as a doctoral student was health policy. So I see the role of government in communicating about health and the role of us in communicating with government about our needs.

As a woman, I experience my own health and health care based on the many ways that health and health care have been aligned with reproductive health for women. But as a woman whose father has had triple bypass surgery, whose husband endures the carryover effects of high school football and a family history of heart disease, whose son typifies hard-working computer engineers in the twenty-first century – 60-hour work weeks with time beyond that devoted to email and online work – squeezing in a basketball game when possible – and whose grandson is at risk for diabetes as he set the record for birth weight in the family (10 pounds, 6 ounces), I have plenty of exposure to how communicating about health is framed for males.

Like most of us who have lived into their 50s, I have relatives who've had cancer, high blood pressure, infertility problems, workplace injuries, and accidents. Some of them have died from these events. Some of them lost gainful employment through no fault of their own. I have seen family and friends buckle under delays related to their injuries, losing their jobs and being caught in a "sport" where bigger is better because there are more lawyers and more money, so bigger can hold out longer. They shape how I come to view roles for health policy and economics in communicating about health.

As an undergraduate, I completed a course in technical writing as part of my major associated with English. That course took me into a health care setting to write a technical report about the Arizona Health Care Cost Containment System (AHCCCS) – a program designed to provide health care to those who meet strict guidelines related to income. That was my introduction to how important income is in the health care equation. For two decades, I've been conducting academic research relating to communication about health and health care, looking for the gaps in communication and ethical strategies to bridge these chasms, as well as exemplars of habit-forming communication. I am not a physician, economist, lawyer, epidemiologist, or any of the myriad of other professionals contributing bits and pieces to the dialogue around health and health care. I often work with all of these professionals, however, and understand and respect the need for us to work together.

Many people have been instrumental in forming my outlook about the importance of communicating about health. My first introduction took place the summer after eighth grade when I assisted Dr. and Mrs. Wagner in his home clinic. I remember most vividly holding a crying infant who had fallen on the wire handle of a bushel basket which punctured the child's face. My job was to comfort the child, and I observed Dr. Wagner comfort the parents. In high school, I was a debater. It was the end of the 1960s. The significance of politics in all kinds of decisions took hold for me, and my lifelong friendship with Mollie and Mary Kahl began. For any college undergraduate, having a mentor can make all the difference in finding one's path. For me, this was Dr. Hank Ewbank who guided me to communication science and my lifelong passion.

I am a professor teaching and conducting research relating to communicating about health and have been for decades now. I have some invaluable colleagues who've supported my passion and pursuits. Celeste Condit was a mentor to me as I entered the field and remains so today. Teri Thompson, as editor of the journal, *Health Communication*, nurtures the talents of many new researchers in the field as she did me. Maureen Keeley and I formed our unending bond in graduate school and continue to champion each other's careers. Jon Nussbaum's enthusiasm for my work has inspired me to continue it. Michael Hecht encouraged me to make the move to Penn State where I've found time and resources to do this work. Kathryn Peters put a genetic counselor's lens over the writing in this book to comment on its validity. My friends, Becky Cline and Denise Solomon, see to it that I take a break now and then. And my family, whom you will meet in these pages, all agreed to enter onto this stage, for which I am grateful. I've had super support from my editor, Elizabeth Swayze, and unending attention to details from Annie Jackson and Margot Morse at Wiley Blackwell. To all, I am appreciative and hope you will be as well in making the journey through this book.

Finally, I am always reminded by my students, both undergraduate and graduate, that what health means is personal for each of us and a lot of factors contribute to each person's assessment. I have been teaching health communication courses to undergraduate and graduate students for two decades as well. A few of the graduate students with whom I've shared the most conversations related to talking about health are Janice Raup-Krieger, Kami Silk, Khadi Ndiaye, Amy Chadwick, and Nichole Egbert as well as Ashley Duggan, Christie Ghetian, and Karyn Jones. The one who got to listen to me talk about this book endlessly and even read and commented on an early draft, Julie Volkman, has been especially encouraging in telling me that this was worth doing. Each of these women is making her own unique contribution to our understanding about why communication about health matters.

The undergraduate and graduate students I've taught have ranged in age from early twenties to late forties and older. Their backgrounds have varied between growing up in rural south Georgia, Pennsylvania, or Arizona, to urban living in Atlanta, Philadelphia, Pittsburgh, Tucson, and Phoenix, to international settings including Senegal, Africa. Their experiences have ranged from never leaving their small hometowns until entering college to traveling throughout the world, and living abroad. The religious backgrounds are varied, as are the cultural traditions relating to health and health care. But all of them have the same motivation for doing what they do as I have. We hope to improve how we talk about health and the choices we make, so fewer of us find ourselves with any regrets linked to our decisions. We hope you will be motivated to read this book and apply it in ways that bring that same benefit to you and your family as well.

1

Why Communicating about Health Matters

As the daughter of a career military man in the US, I never had to worry when I was growing up about whether my family could afford to take me to the doctor or whether a doctor was available. In the US, the federal government has the power to regulate commerce with foreign nations and tax for the general welfare. So the military and their dependents receive basic health care to satisfy the nation's economic aims. Just because I had access, however, doesn't mean that I spent much time at the doctor's office. In fact, I learned the same lessons that most people learn about going to the doctor. Make an appointment and then, "show up and shut up." By following these rules, I also learned what most others would agree with. It can all be a little embarrassing, so we don't talk about it much.

I remember well what it was like to get a school physical. Not much different than the way the movies depicted it for military recruits. The kids in my school were bussed to the military hospital and lined up in this large sterile brightly lit area. We got undressed with girls on one side of a long curtain and boys on the other. The doctors moved along the line to examine us, after which there was some pronouncement such as "good," and then "next." I hoped for a "clean bill of health" and that no one saw me naked while the doctor checked me out. I don't remember ever having a conversation with one of those doctors, unless perhaps to nod or shake my head – if that counts.

I didn't think much about having a role to play in talking to doctors about my health. After all, the doctor couldn't even hear me when using a stethoscope, so why bother talking. They had all those mystical and magical tools, x-ray pictures of my insides and lab studies of my blood. I carried my naïve notions into my civilian adulthood. It was then that I began to realize why communicating about health matters. When first presented with a medical form asking about my family health history, I couldn't answer many of the questions. Cancer? Heart disease? Diabetes? All formed part of my health heritage, but the who, how, when, and where parts of the stories didn't come so easily. I just often didn't know. So I mostly maintained a "cloak of silence" during my medical appointments, speaking when spoken to, avoiding eye contact, and keeping it all as private as possible. Just like the young girl who stood in line to get her physical, practically naked, I wished for a "passing grade" on my health status.

Years later, after I'd married and given birth to two children, I realized how literally life-threatening my attitude could be. As I began to do research in which I listened to doctors and patients talking about health, I formed an appreciation for why doctors and patients behave as they do. We're really all caught in the "eye of the storm" swarming around all the talk about health, trying to make sense of it in the best ways we can. Doctors can't possibly address it all with us in the time they have for our appointments. We don't know what are the most important details about our health to reveal. Over time, I realized that all the talk is affecting our sense of who we are and who's responsible for health. It guides us and government to make decisions about how much time and money to devote to health. It forms our understanding, and sometimes our misunderstanding, about health. It leads us to make more and sometimes less effort, to feel good and sometimes bad, and to make excuses when we don't do what we know we should do. These effects emerge out of talk about health relating to six questions: "Am I normal?" "What are my risk factors?" "Why don't we get care?" "Is acting on public messages about health good for me or just good for society?" "Who makes a profit from my health?" and, "What's politics got to do with it all?" With a little practice, the consistencies and conflicts to be found in all the talk about health can be sorted out. We can decide for ourselves what to act on and what to leave behind, recognizing that these decisions frequently will be based on our overall sense of self and answers to the question, "Who am I?"

It Answers the Question, "Who Am I?"

How we define our *self* connects to communicating about health.

When you answer the question, "Who am I?", a long list of roles and even values are probably part of your response. Talking about health also forms an endless list of possible answers to the question, "Who am I?" Visually impaired. A vegetarian. A runner. An alcoholic. Diabetic. Cancer survivor. Disabled. Pregnant. Impotent. Addict. If we don't have personal experience with a condition, news and entertainment media, including our favorite primetime dramas and many movies, present images to form our understanding. Mary Tyler Moore is internationally known for her ground-breaking roles in TV series aimed at showing women in independent roles. She also manages living with diabetes in her personal life, a role model of independence. Magic Johnson, internationally identified as a basketball player par excellence, also assumes an identity linked to living with HIV. Ronald Reagan and Alzheimer's. Christopher Reeves and spinal cord injury. Michael J. Fox and Parkinson's. However we describe our health, the meanings linked to it have to fit into all the ways we define our "self." But these connections are seldom simple. Take "the smoker," for example.

My father, a Korean and Vietnam War veteran, smoked when I was a child growing up. This was not unusual. My husband's father smoked as well. Both men began smoking during their military careers. My father-in-law began when he received cigarettes in his K-rations as a US Marine during World War II. My father began smoking when airmen got breaks to "smoke 'em if you've got 'em." If you didn't have "smokes," you didn't get those breaks. Since all the fathers I knew smoked, and some mothers did, too, I didn't think much about it. At the time, it was an affordable pleasure. As medical research began to link smoking to infertility, lung and other cancers, heart disease, and a host of health harms, communication about smoking and health formed an identity around being a "smoker." A smoker is someone without the willpower to safeguard their own well-being by quitting, stressed out, frenetic; at best, mindlessly addicted. Or, as the billboard along a US highway pictured in Figure 1.1 claimed, "A 'butt' head." This public health message played on the burned-out ends of those tobacco sticks – butts

Figure 1.1   Photograph of a billboard placed along a busy highway in the US, taken by the author.

– filling an ashtray atop a young man's head. But there are also those media images of smokers which include a rugged individualist sitting atop a horse and that "can never be too thin" actress in our favorite movie or TV series. These competing images may help to explain what has been called "phantom smokers," people who smoke occasionally, but don't want to be identified with the label "smoker." So they don't answer, "Yes," when asked by their doctors on health history forms, "Are you a smoker?"[1]

The identities that form from talking about health affect how, and even *if*, we talk with our doctors, our families, and our friends about health. So both what we *do* talk about and what we *don't* talk about relating to health comes from our sense of how it connects to our self-concept or how it may affect the ways in which we answer the question, "Who am I?" As a result, we're more likely to talk to our doctor about some things even when we aren't asked, because the identity linked to the behavior or symptom is a positive one. For example, being asked about our sleep

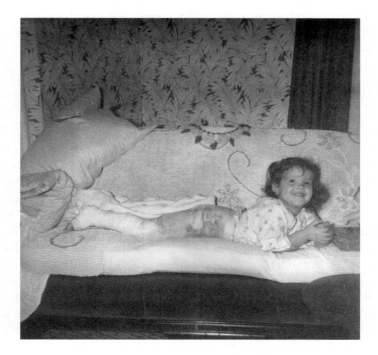

Figure 1.2   Photo of the author at age three with fractured right leg.

habits isn't part of the usual medical interview. But we may tell our doctor we're having trouble sleeping if being diagnosed as an insomniac, someone with persistent problems sleeping, is a sign of being a hard worker. If, however, insomnia is viewed as a sign of being a depressed worker, we may be less likely to tell the doctor about our sleeplessness.

The absence of an identity relating to health may also affect talk about health. I had two children and was well into my thirties before telling a doctor about the broken leg I had as a three-year-old. Family photos like the one in Figure 1.2 and family stories about the event are what I know about it. I don't have an identity related to being "broken bone survivor." Come to think of it, "Have you ever had any broken bones?" has never appeared on those medical history forms. I can think of no images linking broken bones to any of my other roles or, as far as I knew, any of my symptoms across the years. It turns out that having experienced a broken leg at the age of three mattered a great deal and explained many little health problems across the years. But it wasn't until I was nearly

40 years old and developed osteopenia, a mild thinning of the bone mass, in the hip area of the shorter leg that I learned my broken leg grew to be nearly an inch longer than the leg that didn't suffer a fracture. I might have avoided osteopenia if I'd worn a lift in my shoe all those years to counterbalance the force being put on the joint. Of course, that would've meant that I told my doctor about the event, and it never seemed important to do so.

Identities form not just around our health status but also around those who work in health care and the places where care is given. If we get care from a chiropractor, an acupuncturist, a general practitioner, a physical therapist, a physician's assistant, or an internist, differences in their training contribute to differences in how they view health and how they treat us and our bodies. When a certified nurse midwife delivers or assists with the delivery of a baby compared to an obstetrician, women often view their care as more holistic, personalized, integrated, and flexible.[2] When a hospital reorganizes to provide long-term care, social support services, and other programs not usually considered to be part of the hospital, they become a "health care system" – a site for one-stop shopping related to our care. These identities, too, guide our notions of how things will be. And they form our sense of who's responsible, a second reason why communicating about health matters.

It Answers the Question, "Who's Responsible?"

Blame for health comes from communicating about health.

"Why is this happening to me?" "Why can't I get pregnant?" "Why do I have cancer or heart disease?" "How come I'm the one changing my husband's surgical bandages? I'm not a nurse." Our answers to the question, "Who's responsible for health?" emerge from communicating about health. There's tension in decisions about where to draw the line between self and society as being responsible. Smoking illustrates this reality. My father, for example, developed a persistent cough when he was in his thirties, which would have been the 1960s. The military doctor said it might be linked to his smoking. There was, however, no advice to stop the habit. When Dad was on a tour of duty in Guam during the Vietnam War era, he had some particularly bad episodes of coughing. This time a military doctor told him, "Quit smoking or die." My father quit. He smoked a pipe occasionally for a while after that, but the pipes eventually disappeared from our family home as well.

As the science evolved linking smoking to lung cancer and other health harms, smokers began to be told to quit, first by their doctors, then through public health messages, and increasingly from family and friends. Smokers were blamed for their poor health caused by their smoking. Over the years, however, evidence mounted to show that tobacco companies knew that their product was both harmful to health and addictive. Awareness that nicotine addiction challenges efforts to quit smoking shifts some responsibility and stigma from smokers to tobacco companies. These companies also developed identities ranging from "monstrous," to "shameful," and "unethical." And because companies hid the evidence of health risks, consumers lacked information to make informed choices about their health and smoking. Smokers and their families blame the companies and seek some compensation to balance such deception.

Communicating about health and responsibility builds our under-standing of both personal and societal responsibility for health, and our beliefs about whether we have control over our health. Behaviors like exercise, eating, and alcohol consumption are all ones over which we have some control. When research finds that people living in areas with lower forest coverage in Japan have higher rates of cancer compared with people living in areas with higher forest coverage,[3] we feel less in control. If deforestation contributes to increased risk for cancer, we don't really have any alternative to reduce our personal risk through our own behavior. We can, however, hold society responsible and ask our policy-makers to limit destruction of forests in the future.

Unfortunately, communicating about health too often presents one-dimensional views of responsibility. Bits and pieces of talk about causes and explanations for health sit waiting to be organized into action. For example, who's responsible for more children being obese? Pediatricians? They may play a role by avoiding discussions of short- and long-term negative health consequences of obesity. Children? They eat too much food, too many high fat foods, and get too little exercise to use the food they eat. But who's responsible for making so much food available to kids? While parents play a role in making high-fat foods accessible, they buy what's affordable and accessible on store shelves. Food manufac-turers play a role in producing high-fat food. Public schools play a role in reducing the number of physical education classes. Government plays a role in reducing resources for having physical education classes. Crime plays a role in reducing the safety of children playing outdoors in their neighborhoods or walking to school. Pollution plays a role in reducing the air quality outdoors which often limits recreation. Communication that represents most any health event as one dimensional fails to give us a realistic view of the situation.

Communicating about health should be examined for its tendency to overemphasize personal responsibility *or* societal responsibility. Prenatal care for women, for example, has long been promoted as a strategy to improve the birth outcomes of newborns. To reap the benefit, women must show up for appointments to receive such care. Society bears some responsibility for making care available to pregnant women. Both are necessary to achieve the positive response promised as part of prenatal care. But even this is an incomplete way to talk about the birth outcomes of newborns. The March of Dimes in the US has tried to communicate the reality that "men have babies, too." The behaviors and exposures of men affect the quality of their sperm and thus the outcomes of pregnancies. Men who use drugs or are exposed to some products may find the quality of their sperm affected, with a higher risk of birth defects. The twenty-first-century movement toward communicating about *preconceptional* health represents an opportunity to emphasize a role for men *and* women. But once more, society's efforts will be part of the success or failure linked to promoting preconceptional health. If men experience harmful exposures at work, it will likely take action outside their own sphere of control to reduce the risk. Such actions are seen in policies, for example, which require personal protective equipment to be worn when handling products that pose health harms.

Communicating about responsibility for health sometimes leads to unintended consequences, even when the focus of blame is accurate. Mothers Against Drunk Driving (MADD), illustrates this reality. Established in 1980 in the US as Mothers Against Drunk *Drivers*, the name clearly assigned responsibility for drunk driving on the drivers, labeling those who drink and drive negatively. Drunk drivers became the targets of abuse, taking attention away from the real victims. As a result, in 1984, MADD changed its name to Mothers Against Drunk *Driving*. The focus emphasizes disapproval for the behavior of driving under the influence of alcohol rather than stigmatizing drunk drivers.

Communicating about responsibility and health also frequently forms our sense of who's responsible for care. When my son had his impacted wisdom teeth removed, I was given the responsibility for changing the blood-soaked gauze at the back of his mouth and monitoring his symptoms – including bleeding and fever. When the mother of one of my friend's had a mastectomy, she was sent home the day following the surgery with tubes radiating from her chest, and my friend had the responsibility for draining the tubes. When my niece had pneumonia, my sister was handed a breathing apparatus that she was asked to "sign-out" together with a list of instructions about how often to empty her young daughter's congested fluid-filled lungs. These are not exceptions. These are the rule. Knowledge and technology help us to avoid infection and death from impacted wisdom teeth, suffering and early death from breast cancer, and early death from pneumonia, but it's often our responsibility to manage after-care and follow-up. This illustrates the reality that communicating about health also leads to decisions about the allocation of resources, a third reason why it's so important.

It Opens the Gate for "Resources"

Time, money, products, services, people – all come from talk about health. Or *not*.

What do you do to be healthy? Exercise 20 minutes a day, three times a week. Get six to eight hours of sleep each night. Annual check-ups. Monthly breast or testicular self exams. Daily consumption of water. Communicating about health guides our understanding of where we as individuals and the societies we live in should invest time, money, and other resources to promote health. Stop smoking messages, for example, frequently refer directly or indirectly to the economic costs of smoking. For individuals, life insurance, car insurance, and health insurance rates may be higher for smokers than nonsmokers. Debates about whether society or smokers should pay for smoking cessation efforts are weighted against costs of cancer, heart disease, and other health problems linked to smoking. Should tax dollars be used for nicotine gum or services such as therapy to learn stress reduction techniques?

The resources needed, according to most talk about health, center on money. But there are multiple meanings of money as a resource linked to health. For example, the costs for US employers to treat the effects of employee obesity have been estimated to be $45 billion a year.[4]

Despite these costs, economic models suggest that helping obese employees slim down may cost even more, so few companies are tackling the issue head on. How can this be? In part, it's due to the high employee turnover rate. Many US workers stay at one job only four to five years on average, so a company's investment in their long-term health doesn't benefit the company. No one's talking to US workers about this reality or offering creative approaches to the situation. No one's saying, "Make a commitment to us, and we'll make a commitment to your health."

Novel approaches do exist to address the costs related to health. For example, Japanese workers are reaping the health benefits of companies and government investing in their well-being. Japan, too, has had an increase in obesity that accompanies an era of technology and a culture that rewards being a workaholic. Japanese citizens are also eating less fish, vegetables, and rice than was usual in the past, while consuming more fast food. Among nearly 64,000 male workers between the ages of 20 and 54, rates of obesity were examined in 1992 and 1997. In 1992, 21.3 percent of the workers were obese. Just five years later, 24.7 percent of the workers were found to be obese, a significant increase representing more than 2,000 additional men afflicted with this condition. Among younger workers, the increase was 6.3 percent during the five-year period.[5] Workplaces in Japan offer fitness programs over the lunch hour and *require* employees to get their waistlines measured regularly to track progress. The government has tied costs for the national health insurance to employee obesity, and higher costs for contributions from companies are linked to having obese employees.[6] Japan's approach shows a shared sense of responsibility and cost. It includes a national level, where decisions about how to pay for universal health care for citizens are tied to organizations. It also includes an organizational level, where decisions about how to pay for benefits for employees are tied to individuals.

Talk about health frequently focuses on an economic model of costs and benefits connected to a role for society in allocating resources to health. In the US, the Centers for Disease Control and Prevention (CDC) published a report called, *An Ounce of Prevention . . . What are the Returns?*[7] Bicycle-related head injuries, flu in the elderly, and sickle cell screening for newborns are among 19 issues examined for the number of citizens affected and the cost, compared to the effectiveness of prevention and its cost. Their conclusions reveal what savings in direct medical costs are achieved for each dollar spent. And in cases where there's a net cost, the report considers whether the money invested in prevention reaps value for the investment. They conclude, for example, that yearly mammograms carry a net cost but give considerable value for the money invested. Childhood vaccines, on the other hand, are shown to have direct medical savings for each dollar spent.

Family budgets include many resources devoted to health, both directly and indirectly, which are linked to all the talk about health and prompt some choices in lieu of others. The success of a campaign to get us to eat "five fruits and vegetables each day" depends in part on our having the resources to obtain fruits and vegetables. As we spend a lower percentage of income on food, we are becoming more overweight, with energy-dense foods being the lowest cost options. These include refined grains, fats, and added sugars.[8] Add the cost of recreation and leisure, including food and drink, products for personal care such as toothpaste, soap, and shampoo, and resources to stay warm in winter and cool in summer – it all adds up. My baby book reveals that I was admitted to the hospital for pneumonia when I was five months old. I was born in early September, so that would have been early February – the middle of winter. When I asked my mom about this, she said their apartment had no heat in it. The only source was the oven which they turned on and opened in an effort to bring some heat into the area. It apparently didn't work very well.

Resources go well beyond money, of course, in our efforts to be healthy. Social support, which is our access not only to information but also the tangible things we need to be healthy and the skills to follow through, is a resource persistently found to be of vital importance in efforts to manage our well-being. Someone living with diabetes who should take medication every day, test glucose levels, exercise, and maintain an appropriate diet to manage their health is far more likely to do so with support from family and friends.[9] This is true across conditions ranging from heart disease, cancer, and arthritis to back pain, as well as the need to follow safety rules in nearly all areas of our lives. It's the teen whose parent reminds him or her to wear sunscreen at the pool who's more likely to do so, the worker whose work site has safety posters with the steps to follow in being safe posted next to equipment who remembers to do so, and the public school students whose cafeteria posts the calories and fat grams included in different food options who make better eating choices.

Resources for health also link to the availability of doctors and other care providers, of course, the focus of talk about health all around the world. A lack of doctors is a structural barrier to getting care. Rural areas often face this dilemma. My husband, for example, grew up in Tombstone, Arizona, one of seven children, four of them boys – he the oldest. The family had a ranch made up of 32 sections of land, mostly leased, with one boundary along the border with Mexico. The boys spent countless hours in the hot Arizona sun, sans sunscreen, and without hats. Then two decades later, we spent more than a decade of our married lives living in Tucson, Arizona. During those years, he returned to the family ranch on a regular basis, this time usually wearing a cowboy hat but still without sunscreen. In middle age, suspicious spots on his skin began to appear. Some have been removed, but most recently, the dermatologist observed that he needed to have a complete body skin cancer exam. While we live in a university town, it's in a large rural area and the dermatologist he saw is the only skin specialist. So it took six months for my husband's appointment to be scheduled. As the time for the appointment approached, he tried to move the appointment due to a conflict. The appointment receptionist warned him that there were 60 people on a waiting list for skin biopsies and minor surgeries. "In other words," she said, "keep your appointment and don't count on getting in any earlier. If you cancel the appointment, it will be seven months before we can reschedule it."

Talk about health determines how much money will be devoted to medical research and for what purposes. Arguments that guide how resources will be allocated for medical research are often invisible to us, but have tremendous effects on our well-being. They form the evidence base about "health," both what is known and what isn't known. Funded research in the National Institutes of Health in the US, the National Institute for Health Research within the National Health Service in the United Kingdom, the National Institute of Health and Medical Research in France, and the National Institute of Health in Japan all illustrate this reality. Medical research contributed to evidence to support a link between smoking and lung cancer, for example. Until that evidence was available, disputes continued about such links. Similar debate has surrounded the question, "Does passive exposure to smoke contribute to disease?" Individual, institutional, and societal biases affect what research gets funded, leading to disparities in understanding and care, as discussed in Chapter 7. And, as with the scene in *The Wizard of Oz* in which Dorothy reveals the "great and powerful Oz" to be simply a man behind a curtain standing at a control panel designed to make him appear to be so much more, we frequently feel that someone besides us controls these decisions, someone who knows more and can make better choices. When we realize, however, that both what we know and what we don't know about health depends on these decisions, it's a further revelation as to why communicating about health matters.

It Promotes (Mis)Understanding

Our abilities to understand symptoms, give informed consent, and make informed decisions about health come from communicating about health.

Are you ever surprised, puzzled, or even annoyed by the fact that one message about health says one thing and another message says something quite the opposite? Communicating about health is often misunderstood because the vocabulary is both complex and unfamiliar. The words used are ones that we don't use in our everyday conversations – even when we do talk about health. We say we have a pimple on our face, not a cyst. We say we have a growth on our arm, not a tumor. We talk about family history but don't say "hereditary." Consistently, only about one-third of us are found to know the meaning of these words and others that doctors often use and expect us to know.[10] One of my friends has been dealing with an injured knee and after a visit to an orthopedist, returned to the office upset. She told me,

> He talked about things that were in my records about which I had no awareness. He said I had "repetitive strain injuries" and "a popliteal cyst" – which I asked him to write down so I could look it up later. The orthopedist said these were the diagnosis a couple of times when I had seen my primary care doctor for knee pain in the past. I told him, "I think I would remember if my doctor *told* me I had a cyst." The orthopedist said my doctor might've called it a "Baker's Cyst." It's the collection of too much joint fluid in the back of the knee being caused by inflammation in the knee.

We often rely on doctors to explain medical terms they use when talking to us, but even when they do, many too frequently rely on the use of metaphors. When asked why, doctors say that the difficulty of translating medical and scientific terms is most easily achieved by using language that can be easily understood by lay audiences – metaphors.[11] There's little evidence to suggest that this is the case. In the United Kingdom, for example, among 105 people asked about the meaning of terms doctors use such as "spots in the liver" and "seedlings" to explain the metastatic spread of cancer, only about half understood that they meant the cancer was spreading.[12] Describing the role of genes for health as "a blueprint of our future," is understood by some to mean that genes set an absolute path for our future health, while others see it as meaning that genes are a framework that can be revised or even dramatically reworked.[13]

When our doctors don't explain it and our friends or family don't know either, we often turn to the internet. When my girlfriend and I tried that by entering "Baker's cyst," it resulted in 388,000 hits in 0.08 seconds. The question, "What is a Baker's cyst?" returned 228,000 hits in 0.12 seconds. The first three responses explained that such a cyst is a soft and often painless bump, a closed sac or bladder-like structure that is not normal, and a firm, *walnut*-sized fluid-filled lump behind the knee. "A walnut?" my girlfriend said. "I've never had anything on the back of my knee that was like a walnut." So the same strategies doctors use to translate medical content to us are used in online health information as well.

Communicating about health also causes confusion when it doesn't make intuitive sense. Women's risk for cervical cancer, for example, has been linked to smoking, but women have stated that it makes no sense to them.[14] While smoking and lung cancer are seen as having a logical connection, the same cannot be said for smoking and cervical cancer. Our understanding depends upon our willingness and ability to integrate research evidence that may make no intuitive sense. This lack of integration poses a barrier to thoughts and action. In looking back, and with prompting from an orthopedist, my girlfriend who was struggling with knee pain remembered that her primary care doctor told her a long time ago to get some physical therapy for her knee and that her insurance would cover several visits. "That made no sense to me," she said. "The doctor had told me to limit my jogging, tennis, and biking. Then he says to get therapy to build my calf and thigh muscles." She wasn't making the connection between building those muscles and gaining strength to support her injured knee. She was seeing both as work-outs involving her knee.

Sometimes, science makes different recommendations based on the same behavior having different effects for our health, once more causing the talk about health to be confusing. Sun exposure provides an apt example. As a child growing up, I walked miles and miles of shorelines along the Great Lakes with my paternal grandmother in the summers, leaning over to look into the waters and collect stones as souvenirs, some of them the treasured Petoskey stones with fossil forms etched into their surfaces. I swam with cousins in cold water and then baked warmth back into my body as we had relays on the beach. No one talked about skin cancer yet because there was no science to support a risk due to overexposure to the sun. There was, however, science relating a lack of sun exposure to vitamin D deficiency and rickets.[15] As people began to talk about skin cancer and the sun, I heard my mother express confusion over the conflicting health messages associated with the need for sun exposure to avoid rickets and the need to avoid sun exposure to reduce skin cancer risk.[16] "How much sun is too much sun?" she asked.

Misunderstanding may arise because communication about health reflects the fact that different medical evidence may apply to different people. Some people will *not* be advised to behave in ways that others are, because research didn't include participants with characteristics like their own. These may include biological sex, age, or race. Minors under the age of 18 years, for example, are often not included in research unless the topic is considered to address children's health. As a result, complications arise from the use of some medications or other therapies for them. Media stories have reported about this happening for some medications used to treat depression, for example. Concern has emerged about whether the use of these medications may actually increase the risk for suicide among teens using them. Cold medicine was never tested on children under the age of two, and use has been found to lead to serious and even life-threatening effects.[17] Thus, prescription and overthe counter medications, as well as other therapies, have been developed based on their efficacy with some groups while excluding other groups.

Sometimes new science conflicts with old science and affects our understanding. Too few efforts are made to tackle this head on. I've known women in my mother's generation who say that they were told that the "womb" was a safe place for a baby to grow. Their behaviors like smoking and drinking, they were told, didn't influence a newborn's health. This may help to explain why, despite public health efforts to get women to give up smoking while they're pregnant for the benefit of a child, some women don't. Their mothers may tell them that they smoked and their babies were healthy. Some organizations may make different recommendations relating to our health than other organizations do based on "new" science, which adds to our confusion. Cervical cancer screening guidelines, for example, differ between the American Cancer Society (ACS), the American College of Obstetricians and Gynecologists (ACOG), and the US Preventive Services Task Force (USPSTF).[18] How often to be screened varies, depending on the type of screening used and the organization making the recommendation. With a conventional Pap test, the ACS and ACOG recommend screening annually *or* every 2–3 years for women 30 years of age and older who have had three negative cytology tests, while the USPSTF recommends at least every three years. The recommendations are even more varied when using the liquid-based cytology screening method, with the ACS recommending every two years, while ACOG recommends annually, and USPSTF states that there is insufficient evidence to make a recommendation. For women 30 years of age and older who've had three negative cytology tests, ACS and ACOG assert that every 2–3 years is appropriate. All these recommendations may contribute to women's confusion about when to be screened. All three organizations do agree that screening should be started within three years of onset of vaginal intercourse, but not later than the age of 21.

Our ability to understand communication about health may also depend upon awareness that often there simply is *no* science to guide communicating about health. This isn't because the sample used in research didn't include someone like us. It's because the issue hasn't yet been addressed in medical research. That doesn't necessarily make it unsafe. Just untested. We often don't tell our doctors we use nutritional supplements such as herbs because we aren't asked about it. We often aren't asked because there's no medical evidence to say that nutritional supplements are either safe *or* unsafe for use. Since the study of complementary and alternative medicine and practice hasn't been funded in the same way that biomedical approaches using drugs and surgery have been, questions about use of herbs is a hit or miss process, with little chance that it will be included on medical history forms. In the wake of these realities, it's sometimes difficult to know how to behave in health promoting ways. This can lead to excuses when we don't, and anger when we do and it turns out badly for us, a reality that forms a fifth reason why communicating about health matters.

It Guides Effort, Emotion, and Excuses

The energy put toward health, experiences of positive and negative feelings, and accounts of why we do what we do emerge out of communicating about health.

Have you ever found yourself thinking or saying, "If I'd only known, I would've done it to protect my health?" Regret is just one emotion we experience when we find out that we "could've or should've" when it comes to our health. Communicating about health arouses emotions, some of which are negative. We become fearful that we're susceptible to a health harm. It causes worry and dread.[19] We get embarrassed that, even though we knew better, we did something that caused us harm. Even when I did know the answers to some of the questions on medical history forms, it wasn't so easy to tell what I knew: medications I was taking, their names, the dosage; habits I had. We feel guilty when we eat too much, drink too much, work too hard, or drive too fast.

The effort we and others put into health can be traced back to talk about health, but there are gaps in the talk, gaps in our understanding, and so gaps in our behavior. Communicating about health is frequently intended to promote our efforts to be healthy, but may only create an overwhelming feeling of "can't." Research that included thousands of patients in Australia, Canada, New Zealand, the United Kingdom, and the US has indicated that we all feel much the same way.[20] Large numbers of us are dissatisfied. Our top three complaints? Poor communication with doctors. Poor coordination of care. Medical or medication errors. Poor care coordination, and medical or medication errors have direct links to poor communication. Poor communication thus appears to be all too common.

It's a ghastly dilemma we too often face. We've committed effort to being healthy, but we aren't. We've voted for those who would maintain or promised to implement programs and policies to support health and provide health care. We've given our time and energies to employers who themselves are committed to programs aimed at promoting our well-being so that we can keep on working. We've devoted our income within families to being healthy. And yet, too frequently, it doesn't seem that we've achieved that aim. We know this personally because we *feel* it. We know it professionally because we see it in ourselves and others. We know it as a community because everyone's talking about health and no one's happy about how much it's costing in every kind of resource. Yet, we keep on going in the same directions – long after we know we shouldn't. We keep on hoping to make our effort pay off. We keep on because others including the experts and leaders we've elected keep on. And we keep on because there are only so many hours in a day and we can't think how to do otherwise than what we are doing. Little wonder then that too frequently we feel frustrated, mad, sad, and fearful when it comes to our health, when we should feel hopeful, happy, and glad to be alive.

Talk about health can benefit us in many ways. It acts as a guide for what to do and how to do it. It reinforces the match between our life stage and our mental and physical status. It should allow us to focus our attention on all the other things that matter to us, of which there are many as humans. These are aims that can be realized. It takes intention, however, and a harnessing of our efforts in new ways and new directions. That will be the purpose of this book then, to provide insights to redirect our energies and achieve a better understanding out of all the talk about health, together with improved well-being for ourselves and our societies.

Summing It Up . . .

As I entered elementary school, President Kennedy's Council on Youth Fitness curriculum began to be distributed in the US. A quarter of a million youth were involved in pilot projects in six states – sit-ups, push-ups, rope climbing. There were charts marking the standard and we all aimed for it. My school had a jump-rope contest among other events. I won blue ribbons three years in a row. I learned that both praise and fun increase effort and commitment to physical exercise. What I didn't recognize at the time was that a political leader's agenda contributed to this effort, so that resources were allocated for its support. I also had no awareness of the underlying medical research supporting the importance of physical education and fitness for youth. We were still almost two decades away from the Title IX amendment in the US which supported females' participation in athletic programs in public schools. But I was already well aware that boys played sports and girls were cheerleaders. These gendered identities and roles affected the reality that girls were aiming for records in doing sit-ups, while the boys aimed for leading the count for most push-ups. Across decades of living, being a wife, a mother, a daughter, a sister, and a friend, together with the work that I do relating to how we communicate about health, six questions, sometimes with different answers, emerged at the intersection of these roles in all the talk about health. These form the nexus of why and how we do what we do when communicating about health, whether it's with our doctors, in our families, or among ourselves. In the next chapter, I start with what is perhaps the primary one, the many ways we seek to answer the question, "How 'normal' am I?"

2

How "Normal" Am I?

It was the Fourth of July weekend. I had been to the doctor on Friday and it looked like it would be a while before I would go into labor and deliver my first baby. But on Saturday morning, the pains I was experiencing were different from those I'd had before. These really seemed more intense. And my breathing exercises didn't really help. So my husband and I made the trip to the hospital where we checked in and waited for a while in a "labor" room. But things stopped, as they often do, and we went home. No sooner were we home than I began to have those pains again. This time, I got into a warm bath and tried to relax. I gave it an hour or so, but things were getting too difficult for me to manage. I finally got out of the tub and told my husband, "Take me back. If this isn't the real thing, they've got to give me something for the pain anyway." It turned out to be the real deal.

We lived in a rural area served by a small community hospital. When my son was ready to be delivered, the doctor hadn't yet arrived. When he did arrive, he quickly determined that my son was in distress. His umbilical cord was wrapped around his neck and had been pinched in the birth canal for some time, and he wasn't breathing. It was a very surreal experience to see it all overhead in that big round mirror which reflected back the events that were happening to me. As the doctor delivered my son, he asked the nurse to remove his mask. She began to untie it, and he said tersely, "Rip if off – now!" Only with a bit more forceful language. She did and he placed his mouth over Ben's nose and mouth, literally breathing life into him. Then my son was placed in an incubator and whisked away, before I even got to hold him, to be kept under close watch for some hours to come.

I could see that my son had a bluish color even after he started to breathe. It was very scary. The fear of his not being "normal" stayed with us for years. Whenever something with his health seemed a bit odd, we would wonder if it might have something to do with that early event. Our reaction wasn't unusual. We all generally remember when we or a loved one have been told we're "normal" or not based on what a doctor says or some lab test results, or even in comparison to a news report about someone else's experience or the experiences of our favorite TV primetime characters. Our understanding of "normal" is based on statistics, stories, and even reports that some conditions of "poor" health are widespread. How we think about "normal" also includes understanding how we take care of our health compared to what others do, and the times when we don't want to know how our health compares to "normal." Since efforts to answer the question, "Am I normal?" rely on a nearly limitless use of numbers, that's a good place to begin thinking about how all the talk about health answers that question.

Compared to the Numbers

Don't try to make all the numbers add up. Do keep track of the numbers that are important to you for understanding your health status and treatment options.

Do you know any numbers about your health? Anything besides perhaps your height and weight? At birth, these stats include length, weight, and something less frequently passed along to family and friends called to tell the good news of a child's birth, an APGAR score. This is collected in the US, Germany, France, and Spain to assess the newborn's appearance, pulse, grimace, activity, and respiration.[21] At the time of my son's birth, I'd never even heard of an APGAR score. My son was born with an APGAR score at one minute after birth of just 3. This was based on his blue-gray color, lack of breathing, and absence of reflex. Because this led to immediate efforts to resuscitate him, by 10 minutes after birth, his score reached 8, with 7 to 10 being "normal."[22]

Some of us prefer numerical information, enjoy work that requires the use of numbers, and find numerical information to be useful in making decisions.[23] The numbers used to communicate about health aren't often on a 1–10 scale like an APGAR score. Instead they rely mostly on percentages, population comparisons, proportions, and ratios.[24] Since we deal with percentages in many other areas of our lives, we've become quite practiced at translating them based on a relationship to 100. When we hear "50 percent," for example, we probably translate that to mean "half" – half as likely to die from heart disease or half as likely to benefit from a cholesterol-lowering drug. This may be accurate and help us understand our health status. But it's sometimes inaccurate and misguides our judgments. One thing's for sure, if we try to get all the numbers to *add* up, it's a very frustrating business.[25] We may be told, read online, or hear in the news that being over the age of 50 doubles our risk for some diseases. Being sedentary may double our risk for some diseases. Living in an area where there are no parks to walk in and no safe cycle trails to bike on may double our risk for some diseases. Start trying to add it all up and the number may look like we have a 1,000 percent chance of getting heart disease! That makes little sense and doesn't help our efforts to decide if we are "normal."

Numbers are used not only to describe our current health status but also to predict our future health. Our ability to understand the numbers used to show how far from or close to "normal" we are depends upon making comparisons to some standard often presented as a reference range. There may be different reference ranges for younger as compared to older, for men compared to women, and even for more fit versus less fit adults when a comparison is made. For example, an average or "normal" pulse rate for most people is about 70 beats per minute, a number you may think about when the nurse or technician takes your pulse at a medical check-up and tells you it is 68. My daughter is a runner, however, and for her, a "normal" pulse rate is 55.

We too seldom find out what the standard is to which we're being compared when given numbers to describe our health. Instead, we just remember whether the number was "normal" or not. When I began to struggle with my cholesterol more than a decade ago, for example, my lab results showed that I had a total cholesterol, reported in milligrams per deciliter, of 202 and that less than 200 mg/dL was the "normal" reference range. My triglycerides were in the normal range with a score of 91 and a reference range of 30–200. My HDL or good cholesterol level was in the normal range with a score of 68 and a reference range of 39–96. But my bad cholesterol or LDL level was right on the borderline for high, coming in at 127 when the range was 0–130. The lab report noted that the reference range was based on a study in which the patient population was 49 years of age or older. I was a bit younger than that at the time, so the doctor talked about what that meant for my risk level by comparison to the standard.

As suggested by the reference range for my cholesterol report, age is often an important part of the standard. Health history is also important. Doctors and nurses frequently try to get us to pay attention to both in order to understand what the numbers mean. Too often we don't. In one study, even when nurses told men to *only* consider their cholesterol results in light of both their weight and health histories, the men mostly only recalled whether they were told that the number was in the "normal" range. And they translated that to mean "normal" health.[26]

Besides telling us something about our current health status, numbers are used to form estimates of our health risk. For example, a doctor might say that a woman's chance of developing breast cancer in her lifetime is 1 in 8 and a man's chance of developing breast cancer in his lifetime is 1 in 100. This is called a baseline level of risk. It defines "normal" risk. So it's "normal" for a woman compared to a man to have a greater risk for developing breast cancer. When "normal" risk is high, as it is for women and breast cancer, medical research often focuses on understanding and reducing that "normal" risk. For example, what behaviors might women adopt to reduce risk? Research also focuses on what increases risk. What exposures might cause some women to have an even higher level of risk than is "normal" among women?

It's easy for us to lose sight of the meaning of numbers used to communicate about health risk, because some numbers get lost in the translation. Let's imagine that a news report talks about the risk for breast cancer. Perhaps it reports "Risk in men and women is doubled by being obese." If a woman's risk for breast cancer is doubled by being obese, her risk goes from 1 in 8 to 2 in 8. Doubling a man's risk means it goes from 1 in 100 to 2 in 100. If all that we're told is that weight doubles the risk for the disease, it's difficult to know what that means in terms of how much effort or worry to develop about our risk.

The use of numbers to talk about health risk sometimes uses the expression "absolute risk" which defines the *proportion* of a group affected by a disease in an entire population. In women, for example, 1 in 8 is the proportion of women from the entire population who will develop breast cancer in their lifetime. As with the reference ranges aligned with medical test results, many variables might affect our health risk.

Among a group of eight female friends, therefore, it's not accurate to say that one of them will develop breast cancer in her lifetime. Among a group of women living in one area compared to another area, or women in one age group compared to another, or women who eat a different diet compared to others, the risk may be higher or lower. This fact may be communicated by a number which gives us the proportion of women affected, but we often lose sight of it. In one survey of 2,000 women, for example, almost two thirds incorrectly believed that the lifetime risk for breast cancer applied to their specific age group.[27] These women applied the wrong reference group in efforts to consider their risk. Some complex mathematical models take into account many variables linked to a disease and provide a final estimate of risk.[28] Even they cannot include everything. It just isn't possible. That doesn't mean, however, that numbers don't matter.

The use of numbers to talk about health risk also uses the expression "relative risk." This is a ratio formed by comparing risk in two different groups of people. Risk for men versus women is often compared. If among 100 people at risk for spinal cord injury, of whom 50 are men and 50 are women, let's say 15 men and 5 women develop such injuries. Risk in men is 15/50, while the risk in women is 5/50. The ratio formed when comparing these two groups is 15/50 divided by 5/50 which equals 3.0. Three times as many men as women develop spinal cord injuries in a year in this fictional example. That sounds like a lot of risk for men, and it is. But perhaps not so much because of the comparisons to women per se, but because of the actual numbers or percentage of people affected, 33 percent of men. That's one in three men, or 33 out of 100 men. Our overestimation of risk based on presentations of relative risk often occurs because we forget that conversion step in understanding the meaning of the numbers.

It's not just our risk for developing disease that depends on our understanding of the numbers. Our decisions about what treatment to choose are based on numbers as well. In one study of 100 Australian women diagnosed with early stages of breast cancer, for example, more than half of the women couldn't calculate the possible *benefit* of having additional, or adjuvant, therapy relative.[29] The women were told that 30 percent of women with a cancer like their own would have the cancer come back within five years. This is the "normal" risk linked to the chance of recurrence. The women were also told that additional treatment could reduce the risk of recurrence in five years by 30 percent. The recurrence rate for those who receive the additional therapy thus would be reduced to 21 percent within five years. This is arrived at by calculating 30 percent of 30 percent ($0.30 \times 0.30 = 0.0900$). Since 0.09 equals 9 percent, we then subtract 9 percent from the 30 percent to arrive at 21 percent. This correct answer was given by 47 percent of the women. That means that more than half the women made a decision based on *inaccurate* understanding. In fact, 28 percent of the women believed that additional treatment would reduce risk of relapse to zero – a problematic expectation. Not only does this lack of under-standing contribute to a *less* informed decision, it's also likely to increase dissatisfaction with health care.

One reason that numbers are used to communicate about health is the belief that they project an impersonal or neutral voice. That's sup-posed to help us avoid feeling anxious. But many of us feel anxious about any message that relies on our math skills to be understood, however, and our anxiety may make us not even try to understand.[30] The more anxious we feel about trying to apply math to understand, the less confident we become in our ability to apply numbers to make health decisions.[31] As with all skills, practice increases confidence.[32] Our abil-ity to make informed choices about our health may be enhanced by our understanding numbers used to communicate about health. There's a lot more to the human experience, however, than the "law of averages," so to speak. We also often rely on stories to help answer the question, "Am I normal?"

Compared to the Stories

Realize that "nothing more than feelings" is what we often use to make health decisions. And remember, everyone has a story, even more than one.

Have you ever thought about how often you make a decision to do something about your health based on someone else's experience? Exercising because a friend told you it gave him more energy. Getting a colonoscopy because your colleague told you that the technicians are really kind and do everything they can to make you comfortable during the procedure. When it comes to our health, we want to know how medical tests feel, whether they'll pinch, poke, smash, be cold or hot, make us bleed, or make us forget. And we want to know if what we *feel* is "normal."

Stories, unlike numbers, are personal. They present involved rather than detached views of risk. They describe how an experience felt. Numbers might occasionally indicate *how many* of us report feeling fear or guilt or some other emotion in response to a diagnosis or lack of compliance with a recommendation. Numbers can't convey how it *feels* to feel that way, or what to think or do in response. I'll never forget, for example, the terror I felt as a mother when one afternoon, I received a phone call about 4:30 from my son-in-law. My daughter was about to be transported to the emergency room of a nearby hospital with the likely diagnosis of blood clots in her lungs strangling the very life out of her. It's hardly the time to be logical when your child is fighting for her life. I felt that some kind of mistake must've been made and even argued with my son-in-law. My daughter hadn't been experiencing such classic symptoms for blood clots as leg swelling or pain. We knew about these signs because my family had more than one "story" linked to blood clotting based on our experiences. My father, who served as a B-52 bomber crew chief in the military during the Vietnam era, made many flights crouched in tight quarters for long periods of time and, as a result, experienced blood clots in his legs. One of my younger sisters experienced blood clots in her legs from the use of birth control pills. Neither had experienced clots breaking off and traveling to their lungs, an often fatal event.

While numbers give us insights about our health when compared to some statistical standard, stories reveal the meaning of "normal" by telling us how signs and symptoms of good and poor health are experienced. We usually tell stories to describe events that disrupt our life routines. Stories about health frequently include a time stamp, such as "when I was pregnant," or "when my dad had bypass surgery," or "the first time I had sex," "the first time I got a physical exam," "the first time I had a tooth pulled," "the first time I took pain medication," and "after I started chemotherapy," "after I gave birth," "after I had a vasectomy." We often *think* in stories and use autobiographical reasoning to understand and make decisions.[33] To understand a story, we link it to our own experiences.[34] This makes it crucial when we're comparing our own health status to another's for us to be aware of *whose* story is being told.

Stories about health come from many sources and may even include legal testimony or medical histories, but almost always represent a particular point of view.[35] Some stories represent organizations rather than individuals. These *official* stories come from organizations such as the Centers for Disease Control and Prevention (CDC) in the US, for example, keeping us informed about how common conditions such as flu and uncommon conditions such as anthrax exposure are affecting individuals and communities. These stories may appear as news reports featured locally, regionally, nationally, and at the organization's internet homepage, to give us a sense of what "normal" threats exist to our health at a given point in time. Other official stories come from health care organizations, including hospitals, to explain readiness to address possible health threats or as a response to a patient's experience. Because we so often rely on stories to guide our understanding, many organizations have begun to provide access to firsthand accounts which have been prescreened for their accuracy related to medical details. The American Cancer Society, for example, includes stories of cancer survivors on their internet site.[36] These might be described as "official" firsthand accounts.

Firsthand stories, like my daughter's in Table 2.1, form many of our expectations about "normal." Stories from family and friends about their experiences form our expectations about "normal" transitions across the lifespan relating to physiological changes which range from hearing, seeing, and even breathing, to age of onset for menstruation and nocturnal emissions, and "normal" experiences relating to diagnosis and treatment. Newly diagnosed cancer patients' stories about their experiences, for example, reveal that having more than one doctor was "normal." Negative reactions to this truth were also "normal."[37] Telling our stories about our health experiences help us to cope with them. Cancer patients receiving radiation therapy for breast or prostate cancer, for example, adapt better physically, socially, and vocationally when they share their experiences of pain, fear, recurrence, financial concerns, treatment side effects, and even death.[38]

Telling firsthand stories may help the teller to cope but may also form deterministic views of "normal." In one study of 551 firsthand birthing stories, for example, women shared how the fear that they experienced during childbirth reduced their participation in decisions about pain medication.[39] Hearing such stories may help women be better informed about how "normal" it is to experience fear during childbirth. But they

Figure 2.1   The author's daughter, Joy Smith, a collegiate rower and award-winning crew team coach.

may also decide that it's "normal" not to participate in decisions about pain medication.

Secondhand stories are also common and form our understanding of how "normal" our experiences are in such implicit ways that their effects may be harder to identify. In one study of 132 breast cancer patients, women revealed the implicit effects of secondhand experience stories, as 49 percent said that they did *not* disclose their worries about the diagnosis because they had concerns about money, about missing opportunities with family, and about being disfigured.[40] *None* of these women had personally experienced any of these issues firsthand. Based on others' stories, however, the women formed expectations that the financial cost, whether it included lost wages or child care or other matters, the time invested, and threats to personal body image were "normal" outcomes related to their diagnosis. These expectations formed barriers to their own responses in the situation.

While firsthand and secondhand stories often occur through conversations with our full awareness that someone's sharing a personal experience, *invented* stories comprise a vast area of communication that affects our understanding of what's "normal" regarding health. These come from all forms of entertainment media and affect what we expect as "normal" ways to look, feel, and behave when it comes to our health.

Table 2.1 Joy's story about her experience with pulmonary emboli from use of oral contraceptives.

To: Tracey@q100atlanta.com
Subject: Peachtree Roadrace
Dear Tracey,
I was listening to the Bert Show Monday morning, and I heard that you were looking for people with inspirational stories about why they would like to run the Peachtree Road Race. I've never entered a radio contest, but I think that this is a good one for me to try. I'll try to just give you the highlights of my story, because I'm sure that you have to read a lot of these things . . .

I think that I knew something was wrong, long before I admitted it to myself. I'm one of those women who has so much on her plate, the thought of slowing down for anything is almost unimaginable. It was this past February that I started to think that something might be wrong. I ran in a Peachtree qualifier. Women have to finish under 55 minutes in order to start a bit ahead of the pack on Peachtree Saturday. I have never been a super runner, but that time shouldn't have been a problem for me. I ran the race in sheer pain and crossed the finish line 42 seconds away from qualifying. I was upset with myself for getting out of shape, but committed myself to trying again. Over the next couple of weeks, despite my effort, I became more and more exhausted and strained with every workout. I blamed my fitness; I blamed my allergies; I blamed my hectic schedule. I thought of a million different causes for my declining fitness. Finally, things took a rapid downhill turn. I began having pains in my chest and pain from breathing the moment I rose from my bed in the morning. I coach a high school rowing team, and one of my rowers came down with pneumonia. I assumed that I had the same. My husband finally made me go to the doctor, and they ran a battery of tests. My fitness was good (I had been an athlete in college), and my lungs were clear. Still, the doctor had a suspicion that I had a blood clot in my lung, and I needed to get to the hospital right away.

We drove to the hospital, but I was so frustrated because I felt like this would not be anything serious. We were wasting time; I had so much work to do at home. We had a wonderful nurse who sat with us and made us feel pretty comfortable in the emergency room. They wheeled me off to have a CAT scan of my lungs.

I returned from that and relaxed for another 20 minutes or so, until the doctors came in. I could tell right away that something was wrong. Wes wasn't smiling anymore. They told me that I had extensive clotting in both my right and left lungs, including a blockage off of the pulmonary artery. The condition is called pulmonary emboli and one clot to the lungs is frequently fatal. My lungs were just filled. I knew that I was sick right away. I was immediately hooked up to monitors, IVs, and oxygen, and I began to cry.

Table 2.1 (*cont'd*)

My poor newlywed husband of three months went between comforting me, relating the information to my parents and his, and dealing with his own shock and horror of the news.

I was a very lucky woman. Because I had such a great lung capacity from being a collegiate athlete, I could handle the clotting and still maintain plenty of oxygen to my system. The hospital was hard to sleep in, and I wanted to go home so badly. They let me go home after a couple of days, but I had to give myself shots in my stomach of blood thinners every day for 10 days. The first two weeks were VERY rough. My parents came down from Pennsylvania, and friends and family came to help. I was just so tired. I don't know how I had been keeping up. The doctors said that the clots had been massing for weeks to months. It was almost two months later before I was given the ok to exercise again. I was horribly out of shape, and a little scared of being able to tell whether being short of breath was just due to the exercise or my lack of lung capacity. I have a wonderful friend named Jenny who became my personal trainer. Cell phone in hand (in case of emergency), she ran/walked alongside of me, helping me to build back up. It was painful at first, but I have come such a long way at this point. Needless to say, during all of that, I missed the registration for the Peachtree Road Race.

At the time, I didn't believe that I would be able to run it. However, I feel that completing the Peachtree would make me feel that I had overcome the physical barrier that has been holding me back. Since I have been working out, I have had a stress-test performed on my heart, and I am completely clear for all physical activity. I would love to have the chance to run the Peachtree Road Race with Q100.

I'm sorry that I didn't manage to keep the story more brief. I really appreciate your consideration of me for the race number.

Thanks,

Joy Smith

Movies affect our beliefs about control over our health, including what access we have to care and how such processes as the spread of a virus or the onset of cancer occur. TV shows often portray habits with health effects such as poor nutrition being shown as "normal." In some of our own research, we found that the first message that comes to mind about the role of genes for health is a movie. These included *Gattaca*, *Jurassic Park*, and *Multiplicity*.[41] *Gattaca* focuses on the story of a world in which babies are genetically enhanced to eliminate disease. *Jurassic Park* focuses on the cloning of dinosaurs to populate a theme park. And *Multiplicity*'s plot line focuses on cloning to solve the competing demands associated with work and family lives. These invented stories set unrealistic expectations for what's normal when it comes to how medical research about genes and health might be used.

Culturally common stories, which may be told by someone who has no direct or only secondhand experience, are repeated to make an issue or practice salient in a cultural group.[42] Culturally common stories may form beliefs about the appropriateness of having male physicians conduct exams of females or having females touch their breasts, a necessary part of performing breast self exams. Culturally common stories also affect how we view the role of medicine, technology, and science for health, contributing to our beliefs about personal control over health. Over time, some practices repeated in culturally common stories are ones that some members of the cultural group actually experience, allowing them to tell the story firsthand and to reinforce the story's key message.[43] Feelings of mistrust may be shared in culturally common stories as well. African Americans in the US tell about the experience of the Tuskegee Syphilis Study which began in 1932 with recruitment of 399 African American men to study the course of the disease across the next 40 years. There was no standard treatment for syphilis when the study began. By 1947 penicillin was the standard treatment but it was withheld from study participants until the media reported the story, leading to the study's termination. This did not occur, however, before 28 men had died from syphilis and 100 others had died from complications related to the disease. Telling about this event reminds that trust was violated by medical researchers. One cultural story repeated among Mexicans about what was "normal" in relation to their health was that the use of lead for folk medicine and in pottery for so many generations had led them to adapt to it, so that they could take high doses without being harmed.[44] This isn't true, but illustrates the importance of understanding that some cultural beliefs and practices which seem just "normal" to us could pose harm to our health. As a result, we also gain some insights about how something that's an indicator of poor health sometimes becomes "normal."

When It Comes to Poor Health

Be aware of when being "normal" is just an excuse.

Have you ever thought to yourself or even said to a friend or family member, "It's *normal* to be exhausted," or "to overeat when you're stressed," or "to drive around town without your seatbelt on"? There's a tension for all of us between communicating about poor health in ways intended to reduce our own and others' bad feelings about being stereotyped because of our health and *normalizing* poor health or poor health habits. For example, many of us initiate healthy practices, such as flossing after we've just been to a dentist, but slack off not long after.[45] So not flossing is "normal," but it isn't healthy.

Communicating about poor health may reduce our motivation to try in domains of our health and well-being where we actually do have some control. The growing numbers of us with diagnoses of diabetes or obesity, for example, make these diagnoses almost "normal" if defined by the numbers representing the likelihood that it happens. This may reduce the negative labels and stereotypes linked to the condition and behaviors such as overeating and not exercising. It may also increase the likelihood that resources will be allocated to discover ways to manage these conditions. One challenge in talking about health is to encourage people who face these health situations to seek help, but not to feel that it's OK to rely on medical interventions or ignore the health threat because it's "normal."

Normalizing poor health sometimes contributes to our use of health status as an excuse. For example, the numbers of college students claiming to be depressed has risen to such levels to explain absences around exam time, administrations often require certification from medical experts to support the claim before an instructor adjusts timelines based on the student's condition. In turn, students have so saturated experts with requests for these medical "excuses" that a form letter with office logo and a stamped signature is passed out to satisfy the request. In turn, college administrators make more rigorous requirements, with the cycle being potentially unending.

Normalizing a diagnosis can also lead doctors and others to dismiss significant events affecting our well-being. Stress, for example, may be an overused and all too "normal" diagnosis. It tells us practically nothing to have a doctor say, "Well, perhaps it is due to stress." This comment may be in reference to skin eruptions, sleeplessness, loss of appetite, overeating, erectile dysfunction, and almost any other condition we might appear in a doctor's office with. Sometimes, a diagnosis of stress is often a substitute for a doctor telling us that they can't find an explanation for our condition. The word for that is idiopathic – that is, the cause is unknown. My mother, a slender woman as pictured in the next chapter, doesn't have diabetes but still has neuropathy of her lower legs. After efforts to identify a cause were unsuccessful, her doctor said, "It's idiopathic. That means we are a bunch of pathetic idiots who don't know why this is happening to you."

Normalizing pain among the elderly impairs older adults' ability to live quality lives. Most elderly patients are seen by internists and family practitioners rather than geriatric specialists. These doctors often assume that pain is just a "normal" part of the aging process. It's not. Pain experiences of elderly patients are often a sign that something is wrong, just as they are with younger patients.

Normalizing addiction has also appeared in the lexicon – "workaholic," "chocoholic," "shopaholic." This trivializes actual addiction or addictive tendencies. An endless list might be generated of the ways that addiction and addictive behavior have been normalized in this fashion. This, too, harms the impact of a serious diagnosis linked to addiction.

It's also "normal" for our health to be parsed into so many parts that it's difficult for us or our doctors to put it back into a cohesive whole and make sense of it. That contributes to misdiagnoses, missed diagnoses, and lots of frustration in between. At a broad level, we have vision, dental, and medical care just for starters to give a sense of the terrain. As someone who's worn eyeglasses since elementary school and was diagnosed with optic neuropathy some years ago, I've learned that even a specialist in neurology or a specialist in ophthalmology doesn't have the advanced training needed to treat my condition. An optic neurologist is more specialized than either, focusing on just the optic nerve in the eye.

Such specialization is both to our benefit and our detriment. Even when our primary care doctor asks us, "Have there been any changes in your health I should know about?" – time and training limit the likelihood that much more than a notation in our chart will reflect our answer. Perhaps it's not too surprising then that many, if not most, of us search for ways to integrate our well-being across many parts into our lived experience as a whole, leading us to choose alternative treatments.

When Choosing Alternative Treatments

Record the use of alternative or complementary approaches.

What home remedies do you use for your health? Do you supplement your diet with purchases of vitamins? It's "normal" for most of us to choose to use some type of complementary or alternative treatment. Alternative medicine is defined by the National Institutes of Health as something used *instead* of conventional medicine, while complementary medicine is something used *together* with conventional medicine. We choose them because they are accessible, affordable, recommended by friends or family, and they work. I learned to treat bee stings with an onion because I rode on the wagon with my grandfather, dad, and uncles to cut hay, and got in the path of an angry swarm reacting to having their home destroyed as the tractor and plough cut the hay. I remembered that experience when my own daughter was stung by a swarm of bees as we were uncovering patio furniture and stirred up a nest. When I had a colicky baby, I can't count the number of suggestions made to me about how to deal with him. Put some coke syrup in his water. Melt a peppermint and add it to his water. Massage his stomach. Don't eat any spicy food which might leach into my breast milk and cause his upset. Ask any one of us and given a few minutes, we can all come up with lessons learned about taking care of our health that had nothing to do with doctors or schooling.

The use of holistic medicine includes herbal remedies, vitamins, and sensory approaches such as aromatherapy or art therapy.[46] The use of dietary supplements, the most common form of complementary and alternative medicine used by Americans, is a billion dollar industry.[47] Use is influenced by both the numbers we encounter about how many others are using them – making the practice "normal" – and the benefits we hear about from stories. For example, one study of 303 women in the United Kingdom found that supplement users' stories, which often appeared in magazines, led to women's belief in supplements' ability to protect users from possible ill health.[48] Both my parents and my brother use glucosamine, an over-the-counter supplement, to relieve their joint pain. When I began to have some stiffness in my hips, they all recommended this product to me. I asked my doctor about it, and she said that there wasn't much research to support its efficacy, but it shouldn't hurt. I went online and found one study designed to determine the effects of glucosamine use on knee pain. The sample in this study included participants with moderate to severe pain who were 40 years old or older. They were overweight, mostly women, and white. There was significant improvement in pain if they received 1,500 milligrams of glucosamine *and* 1,200 milligrams of chondroitin sulfate daily for 24 weeks when compared to a control group given a placebo.[49] In this study, then, there were several important reference variables, including the amount of pain experienced. In the group experiencing moderate to severe pain, age, weight, gender, and race are all reflected in the results. Among the 1,583 patients overall, the use of glucosamine or chondroitin sulfate alone or in combination did not reduce pain effectively.

In communicating about the effects of glucosamine use as an alternative therapy for knee pain, either conclusion – that "glucosamine works" or that "glucosamine does not work" – would be an inaccurate reflection of the results. The truth is that glucoasmine's therapeutic response depends upon levels of knee pain, weight, how much supplement is consumed, and with what other supplements. The other truth is that there isn't much medical research out there to use in making an informed choice. But there's some. Garlic, for example, has been found to interact with anticoagulants and contraceptives, and ginger with calcium channel blockers, affecting their treatment efficacy.[50] So, while use of complementary and alternative approaches to well-being may be "normal," their interaction with other therapies may be normal as well. In some situations, we will want to know this to prevent harming our health. In other cases, it may not matter to us, as the alternative therapy may be the only option we have. In such cases, we just may *not* want to know how "normal" we are when compared to numbers or stories.

When We Don't Want To Know

Recognize when hope increases danger rather than opportunity.

We don't always want to be "normal" when it comes to our health. As suggested earlier, if it's "normal" to be overweight, we probably would prefer not to be "normal." If "normal" means losing our vision and hearing when we're middle-aged, we'd rather be among the group that isn't "normal," retaining our sight and ability to hear. If we face a life-threatening diagnosis, we would probably prefer to be the exception to a prognosis of death in the near term.

Traumatic injuries, such as spinal cord injuries and brain injuries, are also areas where we just may not want to know what's "normal" in relation to our own health status. The number of persons who survive spinal cord injury (SCI) has increased due to better resuscitation rates, and more available and improved long-term care. More than a quarter of a million people live with SCI in the United States alone, with an estimated two and a half million worldwide.[51] Most of these injuries result from blunt trauma, with the most common source being motor vehicle collisions. More males than females are living with SCIs, and in the US, about half of these incidents occur to people between the ages of 14 and 24. When doctors tell family and patients that they don't have all the answers about the extent of a SCI, our research found this to enhance hope and adaptation.[52] It's especially important for doctors to communicate to SCI patients and their families that fear is "*normal*" as a way to help them cope.

Not knowing what is "normal" based on those charts that forecast risk related to a health condition can also sometimes be a way to promote hope and optimism. Cancer patients whose prognosis is death in the near term, for example, often don't want the numbers and statistics about this reality.[53] Not wanting to share a life-threatening diagnosis is sometimes a "normal" way to protect someone we care about from distress. Researchers in the United Kingdom, for example, asked 270 patients aged 65 to 94 years if they wanted a disclosure of diagnosis of cancer to be given to family and 28 percent said they didn't.[54] Family members may not encourage our talk about illness because they want us to behave as *normally* as possible for our own sake *and* theirs. In one study of family caregivers for newly diagnosed colorectal cancer patients in the US, the caregivers said that the experience totally disrupted *their* lives. So they attempted to stay positive, and keep family and children's routines as *normal* as possible.[55] In another study, men with prostate cancer said that they didn't disclose their diagnosis in order to sustain a "normal" life *and* minimize the burden to others.[56] Unfortunately, not talking may be misinterpreted. Husbands in one study said that their wives didn't need or want to talk about a husband's prostate cancer diagnosis, a belief based on the fact that the wives didn't say they wanted to discuss it.[57]

For some cultures, talking about death is viewed as courting death. While other cultural groups may not hold that view, many still believe that a family member shouldn't be told about a terminal diagnosis.[58] Knowing that death is approaching, however, contributes to families and loved ones having the opportunity to engage in "final conversations."[59] Knowing may also contribute to a greater likelihood of electing high-risk and alternative treatments which present a statistically remote opportunity to extend life but contribute to hope and medical research.[60] So, while it's often "normal" not to talk about the approaching end of life, there are *costs* linked to this practice which warrant consideration.

End-of-life events are also the times when doctors are less likely to discuss "normal" with patients. These events require "breaking bad news." A terminal diagnosis or other serious health finding often leads to a patient's angry response. Doctors have reported that these reactions are detrimental to the patient's well-being and so there's really no benefit in telling.[61] Doctors are, in other words, striving to promote the patients' well-being. In doing so, however, they may remove opportunities for the patient and family to cope with the news.

Summing It Up . . .

We have a significant role to play in communicating about our health to answer the question, "Am I normal?" Being "normal" can bring a sense of relief and calm to our experiences with health, allowing us to turn our attention to other matters. Being "normal" can also give us an excuse not to do the sometimes hard things we need to do to be as healthy as we can be. Either being or *not being* "normal" can arouse anxiety, suggest an identity, lead to efforts to identify the cause, and open a gate to resources. Being normal, on the other hand, may instill a false sense of security, reduce efforts to stay normal, and fail to lead to discussion of resources available to prevent the possible future result of not being normal.

A lot of talk about health aims to guide our assessments of whether we're normal based on numbers and statistics. Our health is more than the sum of its parts but often less than the hundreds of numbers thrown our way to answer the question, "Am I normal?" I can't count the number of times that I'm told, "I don't like numbers," "I'm afraid of numbers," or "I'm not good with numbers" by friends, colleagues, strangers, applicants to graduate school, and students in my classrooms. I can't emphasize too strongly that there's probably no other single thing that will make us more communicatively impotent as individuals than to erect a barrier between ourselves and numbers. It's a foundation for understanding our health status, our health risk, and the possible benefits or harms linked to treatments. It also frames decisions about how much mortgage we want to afford, how many personal and societal resources we believe should be devoted to health promotion efforts compared to medical research, and how worried, fearful, anxious, or angry we get about all of these issues. All of which also contribute to our health.

We should know our cholesterol levels, together with weight, height, blood pressure, and pulse rate, and even blood glucose levels. Each of these numbers about our health status predicts whether we are more or less likely to experience such major chronic illnesses as heart disease, diabetes, or even cancer. Our doctors track them and we should, too. But in doing so, we need to know what standard or reference range defines "normal" and to consider what personal characteristics may contour the meaning of the results. Knowing that different standards describe different people may seem to support the futility of trying to have an active role in the process. In reality, just the opposite is true. Only we have the complete picture of our health, both past and present. Only we can really prevent a misinterpretation of the numbers. And really, only we can keep track of *all* the numbers.

We also need to take stock of just what stories friends and family, media, and even organizations such as the CDC "tell" us about health. Awareness that stories affect us gives us some insights about what information we have implicitly *learned*. We often form our views about whether we have control over our health and whether therapies are likely to work or not based on stories. We frequently learn skills relating to ways to safeguard our well-being not just from the modeling of our family and friends but from the stories of their experiences. Knowing why we believe some things cause disease that we never learned in our science classes and can't find in medical research articles is a good start for explaining how we react to the science of health. Knowing why we refer to some parts of our bodies in ways that we wouldn't find in any of our biology texts is also helpful to predict our ability to comprehend health information. In all these ways, we can take stock of why we feel the way we do when someone starts talking about health habits, medical exams, sex, birth, illness, recovery, and even death. While societies debate the merits of using technology to link our health records, and disasters come and go, we're left in their wake with too little ability to pick up the health pieces – if we don't keep track. In the meantime, and along the way, there are some things we should know about ourselves and why even when we know better, we sometimes risk our health. This requires us to consider the question, "What are my risk factors?"

3

What Are My "Risk" Factors?

My father retired from the military after 20 years and retired again after completing another 20 years as a civil servant. He and my mother wanted time to explore places not yet visited. The two were doing just that, hiking across Alaska as pictured in Figure 3.1, taking their time with respites at secluded bed and breakfast locations, when Dad experienced some chest pains and shortness of breath. They slowed their pace a bit and continued their trip, and he didn't notice any more problems. When they got back home, the pair resumed a more usual pace on the familiar trails around the area where they live, and he again experienced the symptoms. It had to be significant for him to mention it and then to make an appointment to see a doctor.

After a series of tests including a coronary angiogram, my dad was found to have blockage of the left main artery that comes off the heart even before it divides into the left side and the right side, much like the bottom part of the letter "Y," which then divides into two major arteries. The left anterior descending artery, LAD, and right coronary artery, RCA, divide into further branches to supply the front, back, and sides of the heart muscle. The left main artery supplies the entire heart and when significantly blocked, people often do not survive, leading to the blockage acquiring the moniker "widow-maker." Dad received the diagnosis just days before my son's wedding date. He said he wasn't missing the event and told the doctor as much, even though the doctor emphasized the life-threatening nature of my father's condition. My father reasoned that, "I've lived with it this long, I guess I can live with it until I see my grandson married." Of course, he didn't tell any of us that. Only my mother and my youngest sister, an intensive care nurse by training, knew the

Figure 3.1 The author's parents on a hike in Alaska.

diagnosis as they all set out to travel the hundreds of miles between their hometown and where I lived at the time.

In truth, of course, my dad's reaction isn't an unusual one. We all face competing choices linked to living our lives and balancing risks. This chapter focuses on that reality and how communicating about health answers the question, "What are my 'risk' factors?" But it's not specifically about the habits we have which may promote our well-being or the ones that threaten health. Nor is it specifically about how our environments may contribute to health harms. Instead, it considers how and why we act on some content while ignoring other messages that may have more direct meaning for our well-being. The fact of the matter is that communication about "risk," "at risk," and "risk factors" is often not acted on in intended ways by most of us.

We can go a long way in predicting how communicating about health affects us by taking a look at a few personal characteristics. These include how we define reward versus punishment; our need for novelty and aversion to being bored; whether we have a tendency to procrastinate and if so, when? And finally, how central religious faith is to our sense of self and what that means for how we think about our own health. Because responses to reward and punishment cues have innate as well as learned components to them, they suggest a good place to start in answering the question, "What are my risk factors?".

Our Response to Reward Cues

Connect what excites you or gives you pleasure to your efforts to be healthy. Avoid letting your efforts to be excited or experience pleasure cause you health harms.

Does the thought of winning a contest excite you? Do you like to act on the spur of the moment? Maybe you find yourself doing things for no other reason than the fact that they might be fun. I remember going to a party for my husband's company and meeting a couple from Sweden. It was a holiday party and the skiing season had begun. The woman said that she and her husband had been skiing the week before and that she'd signed up for a lesson with the resort coach. When she showed up, he asked her, "What's your goal?" "What do you mean?" "Well, do you want to be able to do the 'Dead Man's curve,' or what?" She said, "I told him, 'I just want to have fun. Is there something wrong with that?' " "You Americans," she said to those of us listening to her story, "always having to have some goal."

We all respond to *rewards*, but what's rewarding for us may differ. My dad, for example, prioritizes family events such as attending my son's wedding. That's rewarding to him and he would risk his health to go after that reward. The ski instructor in using the word "goal" was probably conveying the fact that, as an instructor, he was rewarded by helping those who sign up for his coaching to be better skiers. And the wife of my husband's colleague, by her response, suggests that she is rewarded by "having fun," a rather broad idea that means many things to different people. These are all examples of intrinsic rewards. They can't be directly observed, but guide our thoughts and behaviors nonetheless. A feeling of peace, perhaps of satisfaction in a marriage or a job, and a sense of accomplishment – these are things we may work for, but that others cannot see. Positive communication can also be rewarding. For example, adolescent diabetics manage blood glucose levels more effectively when parents praise them for doing so.[62] This praise makes paying attention to the details of monitoring their levels a more rewarding experience because their parents express appreciation to their children for their effort.

Communication about health often assumes that good health is a reward, in fact, *the* reward. Communicating to us that our risk of getting diabetes has greatly increased because we're overweight is therefore supposed to motivate us to lose weight and achieve good health as our reward. But the message has to compete with why and when food is rewarding to us. So the reward of *not* getting diabetes has to go up against and win over other reward cues, some of which are quite tangible and concrete. Little wonder that so often what seems to be such clear reason to act on behalf of our health isn't sufficient motivation for acting.

We humans are hard-wired, so to speak, with nerves in our brains connected to our body's arousal system. This includes heart rate, blood pressure, sweating, and breathing.[63] These signs of arousal and brain activity are often triggered by rewards.[64] Think about the last time you were feeling rewarded and how that felt. A little faster heart rate, a little rise in blood pressure, perhaps some sweaty palms, and faster breathing. Triggering these events linked to our arousal and brain activity also relates to the release of dopamine. This is a hormone and neurotransmitter that relates to our motivation, pleasure, and the transfer of information in our brains.[65] So rewards are motivating, give us pleasure, *and* spark information transfers in our brains.

When information is transferred in our brains, it affects emotion and cognition. The limbic system in our brains relates to our emotions and the formation of long-term memories. The cortical system relates to memory, attention, and language. Both are affected by the release of dopamine. Thus, our response to rewards, by triggering the release of dopamine, produces pleasure and motivation, and also aids the memory of these experiences. The process even affects our abilities to use language and pay attention. So our response to reward cues has significant implications for how we respond to communication about health and what communication we will be drawn to in the first place.

Some rewards are concrete or tangible such as having or attaining a desired object. This might include money or a new outfit. Some efforts to get smokers to quit smoking have used messages like those in Table 3.1, which add up the cost of buying cigarettes across some specified period of time and point out what tangible objects that we desire could be obtained with the money saved by quitting. Communicating about health also appeals to tangible rewards when weight loss is linked to purchasing a bikini or installation of safety features in our home leads to a better home insurance rate.

Table 3.1   Health information for consumers from the Government of Victoria, Australia.

Smoking – the financial cost

One packet of 25 cigarettes costs around $10.50, and the price keeps rising. If you need an added incentive to quit, think about how much of your pay packet is going up in smoke every week.

What could you do for yourself and your family with that extra money? More than you think. At today's prices, if you smoke one pack of cigarettes per day for 10 years, you'll spend over $38,000 – easily enough to buy a new car.

Source: Smoking – the financial cost. Better Health Channel. Fact sheet. Retrieved from www.betterhealth.vic.gov.au/bhcv2/bhcarticles.nsf/pages/Smoking_the_financial_cost?OpenDocument, on 9/12/2008.

Some of us seek the experience of feeling enthused linked to activating our arousal system for its own sake. Some of us love the excitement of making nerves tingle and hearts race. It's a high priority that guides our actions. The way it *feels* to be elated becomes its own reward and if we have to ride a rollercoaster, drive fast, use drugs, or jump out of an airplane to feel that way, we may do it, all the while not consciously recognizing that riding the rollercoaster isn't what we seek. It's the feeling we get from riding the rollercoaster. That's the reward. Use of an illicit drug or even a prescribed medication may also stimulate the feelings. Exercise may become the "drug of choice" because it's triggering the response we find rewarding, leading to over-exercise. If praise related to our slim physique causes that feeling of elation, how we get there may be less important than getting there, and once there – there may be no idea of being "too thin." Even smokers may be motivated by the feelings which accompany reward experiences, but at a low level of awareness. Nicotine has been found to set off the mesolimbic dopamine system in rats.[66] So perhaps similar experiences occur in humans and subconsciously reinforce nicotine use. Nicotine has been found to enhance human performance on tasks of selective attention, improving the ability to inhibit distracting events or facilitate selective attention.[67]

The links between nicotine use and enhanced selective attention may provide a partial explanation for why some careers seem to align with a greater likelihood of smoking. This includes air traffic controllers.

Perhaps controllers who smoke on their breaks do so partly to increase their ability to focus on the work task, one that demands absolute attention on a narrow scope of airspace to promote the safety of the planes within it. This means eliminating all other distractions, including the sounds of other controllers' voices around them as they perform their tasks. Smoking itself may not be at all rewarding. Yet it may provide a way to achieve what is rewarding, good job performance.

Some individual characteristics are linked to a higher likelihood of seeking reward experiences. Being an extrovert is one. In one study of 2,725 Australians, ranging in age from 18 to 79 years, extroverts were highly motivated to pursue pleasure and feel excited – both rewarding to them.[68] In other research, extroverts have been found to be more likely to engage in unprotected sex and use alcohol in their efforts to experience pleasure and excitement.[69] So, from a health status perspective, extroverts may put their health at risk by engaging in unprotected sex and using alcohol, not because these acts are rewarding but because they produce the feelings of excitement and pleasure which are rewarding. But pursuit of feelings linked to rewards isn't always harmful for our health. In fact, being motivated to be happy is linked to greater openness and sharing, while those who aren't motivated by happiness are more likely to be depressed.[70] This tendency should be considered together with responses to punishment cues, which may be more important, less important, or equally important in predicting an answer to "What are my risk factors?"

Our Response to Punishment Cues

Avoid being "scared to death" because you try to avoid feeling fearful.

Do you worry about making mistakes? Do you worry that someone might be mad at you? Or, do you have few fears compared to your friends? We humans have another system that connects nerves in our brains with our body's responses in ways that affect how we communicate or respond to communication about health. It's aroused by our fear or worry over making mistakes or doing something poorly, as well as the criticism of others. This system is thus triggered by the cues we see as punishing[71] and it, too, predicts what gets our attention. As a result, our responses to punishment cues may contribute to behaviors that put our health at risk, *or* it may guide us to behave in health-protective ways.

Like rewards, punishment can have a wide range of meanings for us, ranging from objects to experiences. We may be motivated by punishments linked to losing a desired object, losing a job, getting a traffic ticket or having to pay higher car insurance, and sometimes, becoming physically sick. Or, we may be motivated by effort to avoid a sense of failure at life or love, or deep dissatisfaction with our job. Punishment, however we define it, relates to our feelings of anxiety, fear, and worry.

Some of us are more motivated than others to *avoid* feeling anxious, fearful, or worried. In the same way that we at times act in order to reap the feelings of excitement or pleasure, we act to avoid the feelings linked to punishment. Some of us experience these as gnawing or skin-crawling anxiety. The way it feels to be fearful, for example, may be viewed as punishment. Anything that might be linked in our minds to the possible experience of fear may be avoided in order to avoid feeling fearful. If speaking in front of a group of people brings that feeling, public speaking becomes an experience to be avoided. If exposure to messages such as the one depicted in Figure 3.2 might produce those effects, we may do our best to avoid such messages. Our effort to promote our health may be compromised by our effort to avoid these messages. Thus, one of the realities we must face is that how we respond to punishment cues is linked to how we approach, avoid, and ultimately respond to communication about health risks.

The human system linked to punishment cues is involved in the release of serotonin, which helps to regulate our aggression, mood, anger, and even sleep and appetite.[72] If the system is overly active, it may lead to serotonin deficiencies. If communicating about health triggers a punishment cue, and we begin to worry and fret about the matter, it may make us more aggressive or angry, cause us to be restless when trying to sleep, or to have a loss of appetite as a result of serotonin deficiencies. On the other hand, communicating about health in ways that reveal possible health threats while showing us that we can handle them may limit the worry and fear we experience. If serotonin is then produced in normal functioning ways, such communication may enhance our well-being, not only through its ability to focus on a health threat and our effective response in handling it, but through its ability to aid our sleep, mood, and appetite.

Figure 3.2 Cigarette packaging label used in Australia. Source: News-Medical.Net (February 27, 2007). Graphic warnings on cigarette packs DO help smokers quit. Retrieved from www.news-medical.net/?id=21764, on September 9, 2008. Reproduced with permission.

We respond to both reward and punishment cues. In turn, the serotonin and dopamine linked to these two systems of response have been found to interact in ways that may regulate our effort in working toward our goals. If one goal is to remain healthy, and it's connected to many smaller goals, such as to eat right and exercise daily, then our awareness of how these systems contribute becomes important. Dopamine activity regulates our ability to perform memory tasks, while serotonin may put the brakes on the activity of dopamine.[73] We humans do all kinds of things to our schedules and lives that interfere with the optimum performance of these activities. Referring back to the example of air traffic controllers, their desire to be competent on the job may be enhanced through nicotine use that triggers the dopamine function in the reward

Figure 3.3 The author's sister on the job in the busy air traffic control tower.

system. Dopamine in turn affects their memory tasks. Short-term memory acuity is vital for professionals who must remember where all those planes are in their piece of the sky at any given moment. Air traffic controllers are infamous not only for their high levels of smoking on the job, but for their erratic sleep patterns. In part, this may arise based on the inability of serotonin to perform its task of putting the brakes on the activity of dopamine.

How might this work to affect health for *all* of us? One of my sisters, pictured in Figure 3.3 on the job, was one of the first female air traffic controllers in a high traffic density tower in the US. Being an air traffic controller requires working a shift that covers the usual nighttime sleeping hours at least once weekly. Then there's a shift that spans the early morning hours at least once weekly. Finally, there's a shift that spans the afternoon and early evening hours at least once weekly.

The master schedule coordinates the controllers' schedules in ways designed to provide them with some consistency around these aims. Thus, a controller may work five shifts starting with a late afternoon into evening shift and backing into the schedule in such a way that leaves the controller working the morning shift, coming home for a quick nap at the time of day when they wouldn't ordinarily sleep so that they can then go back and work the midnight shift. And doing that once a week.

While the schedule is explicitly specified for controllers, its format is one that isn't so very different from mothers who are breast-feeding newborns, caregivers for the seriously or terminally ill, those doctors in training we see in so many primetime shows, or the truck drivers moving products from coast to coast. Communicating with anyone whose life revolves around such a changing schedule about their eating habits, the need to exercise, or other lifestyle choices including smoking may often be met with a bad mood. In truth, it's likely that they can't just "snap out of it." There's been an ongoing debate about how performance may be affected for medical students and doctors, as well as air traffic controllers based on interrupted and erratic sleep patterns. Perhaps if more attention was given to the innate responses going on rather than the levels of our overt response linked to mood or aggression, more serious efforts to revise these activities would emerge.

Punishment cues do sometimes motivate us to behave in a healthy fashion, but perhaps not always in the ways we imagine. Our desire to avoid a punishment and our anticipation of one linked to an action may guide us to approach some paths and avoid others. Among 937 children in third through eighth grade asked about what their parents say relating to "no smoking" rules at home, those who received *more* messages about health risks of smoking and disciplinary action were *less* likely to smoke.[74] The way that the youth could avoid discipline was to avoid smoking. So it wasn't the punishing effects of smoking, per se, it was the punishing cues of parents that motivated them not to smoke. The Australian cigarette package, Figure 3.2, as another example, would be difficult to avoid once the cigarettes were purchased. Thus, to avoid the punishing cues of fear and anxiety aroused by seeing these images, rather than by the health harms linked to smoking, one has to avoid buying cigarettes. This assumes that the images on the cigarette package actually are punishing, which in some cases may not be true.

Just as striving after feelings associated with our response to reward cues can contribute to activities that put our health at risk, striving to avoid fear, anxiety, and worry may also increase our susceptibility to health harms. Again, this occurs at a low level of awareness, until we *decide* to become aware of how much our lives revolve around trying to avoid what makes us fearful. Sensitivity to punishment has been found to contribute to the urge to drink as a strategy to reduce negative states, such as fear, while sensitivity to reward contributes to the urge to drink to achieve positive affect associated with drinking alcohol.[75] Our responses to reward cues *and* punishment cues both contribute to our behaviors. This may explain why, for example, among cancer survivors asked about their preferences for communicating about cancer and recurrence, 43 percent of the participants in one study said that they preferred "70 percent chance of cure," while 33 percent preferred "30 percent chance of cancer coming back," and the rest had no preference.[76] For those of us more motivated by reward cues, "chance of cure" may link to effort and resources to behave in prescribed ways. For those of us more motivated by punishment cues, "chance of the cancer coming back," may better enhance our efforts. For the rest of us, both approach and avoidance tendencies may be equally motivating. It may just depend upon how important having new experiences is to us, another way we may gain insight to answer the question "What are my risk factors?"

How We View Novelty

Avoid being "bored to death" by seeking novelty.

Do you seek new experiences just for the sake of having them? Sensation-seekers strive after novelty and often act on the spur of the moment.[77] Novelty is often a prerequisite for piquing our interest in a topic, but we can carry it too far and put our health at risk. Or we can ignore health messages because they are presented in familiar and even boring ways, using vocabulary that's uninteresting. The efforts to move us from not thinking about our behaviors as having health effects to actually contemplating this reality are more successful when content is novel.[78] But novelty seeking predicts whether we even expose ourselves to content in the first place.

Some of us are highly motivated to seek novel experiences, some of us not so much. Some of us who seek novelty have few inhibitions to limit these searches. Some of us experience this reality in one domain of our lives but not others. Novelty seekers can put their health at risk in efforts to achieve the experiences or sensations linked to their searches for things that are new. It's not a clear path from our responses to reward cues or punishment cues to our novelty seeking tendencies. Some of us are thrilled by the experience of being fearful. An entire industry of horror movies has evolved around this reality. Some of us find it exhilarating to compete in athletic competitions, as suggested by Figure 4, a photograph of Jordan Smith, my son-in law, that expresses his intensity and elation during an international competition. But as my son-in-law reveals in Table 3.2, seeking these novel experiences may put our health at risk.

Some research has shown that the brain and nerve activities that use serotonin as a way to transmit information between a nerve cell and other cells don't function in the usual fashion among high sensation seekers.[79] In other words, there's nothing to put the brakes on when it comes to the nerve tingling gained by activating sensations linked to novelty. High sensation seekers have been found to pay more attention to novel stimuli, including messages or cues embedded within the message content.[80] Among nearly 3,000 midwestern US ninth graders, for example, higher sensation seeking predicted a greater likelihood of having had sex and having unwanted sex when drunk.[81] Adult sensation seekers have been found to be more likely to gamble financially.[82] After all, gambling is, by definition, unpredictable and so every time out is a novel event. In one longitudinal study of how a group of boys developed, those boys who as infants more easily broke visual attention when exposed to the same stimulation repeatedly were followed across time. These boys were found to have higher levels of novelty seeking at the age of 15 years and also to carry one particular version of a dopamine receptor.[83]

Efforts are also being made to gain insights into the effects of communicating about health for those who aggressively pursue novelty. Sensation seekers more often recall a message that has an unexpected ending. Among 25,549 teenagers, recall of 28 Legacy Foundation smoking prevention ads was examined for associations between various message style elements and recall. Use of a "second-half punch," defined as an unexpected end to the ad, was related to a greater likelihood that teens high in need for sensation would recall the ad.[84] Based on such research, the "Singing Cowboy" ad was produced. In it, the man

Figure 3.4   The author's son-in-law, Jordan Smith, 2005 Bronze Medalist at World Rowing Championships held in Gifu, Japan.

dressed as a cowboy, riding a horse down a city street while playing a guitar, removed the bandanna from around his neck to show the hole from his laryngectomy. The song he sings with the help of a hand-held electronic voice box begins "You don't always die from tobacco." The goal, of course, is to increase recall of the ad and also motivate high sensation seekers to avoid smoking either by never starting or by quitting. This illustrates the reality that what may be punishing to some, the fearful view of a cowboy who's had a laryngectomy, is still sought after for its novelty.

What we don't know is whether sensation seekers will still put off quitting even though they recall the unexpected ending. It is, in fact, our tendencies to procrastinate or not that may distinguish acting and just thinking about the need to act, another response to the question, "What are my risk factors?"

Table 3.2 Jordan Smith's story.

Long QT syndrome: an abnormality of the heart; sufferers can be frightened/startled to death, or can suddenly collapse from heart failure (at any heart rate).

In order to play high school sports you have to have a physical. At 15, I went in to have mine and my normal doctor was not there. The covering physician insisted on going through EVERYTHING. She listened to my heart, and asked if there was any family history. One case, I think. Either way something sounded odd. It was enough for her and my parents to warrant a trip to a cardiologist. Since I lost a sister some years back to unrelated problems, they are cautious. The cardiologist put me through a battery of tests, the likes of which were worse than some of my practices. After all the data had been collected they sat down and explained to me what they saw in my test results. They went over all of it with us, explained what a QT wave is, what Long QT syndrome is. Nobody could say what it meant for the future, or maybe they did not want to speculate knowing so little since it had only just been spotted. Of course, more study was recommended.

They sent me to a medical university to see a specialist. As it turns out I ended up seeing a visiting doctor from another country – he had to have a translator. I think translators are supposed to speak both languages, but you could have fooled me. After we got past the fact that I was not going into the NBA the next year, they somehow came to two possibilities (though no more testing or questioning had been done). Either I go on medication that would slow me down mentally and physically but ensure that I would not be frightened to sudden death or hopefully just not collapse one day. Or I could do nothing. Somehow I had the impression that since it was very minor and had not developed into the syndrome that it was going to be OK . . . It was found while chasing a mitrovalve prolapse. The choice to retard myself in that way for a "maybe someday" didn't really seem like much of an option . . . There are a lot of other similar unknowns in life. I have to take this one with a lot of faith. I don't know what it could "do" someday, or if it will ever "do" anything. It was found out of the blue, and it could have easily never been spotted. Do you not chase a dream because of a "what if"?

My heart has been listened to countless times since then, and no one has ever heard or suggested anything out of the ordinary. I have trained with a heart monitor for a year now and never gone outside normal ranges (though I swear I've seen Jesus a few times). I try to live my life. Keep tabs on it, but not focus on it . . .
Jordan Smith

When We Procrastinate

Know that "putting it off" is a decision with health effects, too.

How many times has something relating to your health been on the "to do" list, but it just didn't quite make it into action? The likelihood of procrastinating in relation to any action that we put off doing has been found to be predicted by two things. First, we forget what, when, or why we're supposed to do something. And second, we lack the skills to behave in ways that we know we should. In either case, or for whatever reasons we are putting it off, procrastination leads to more acute health problems. Then, those of us who are procrastinators get caught up in a cycle of not following through on medical advice, knowing we haven't followed through, and so going in for less frequent medical check-ups.[85] In an ever-widening era of expectations that we manage our own health, messages to remind us what to do contribute to our ability to use health information – when we understand it.

Reminders reduce forgetfulness for patients, with use of automated phone calls about appointments long found to increase appointment attendance. Their expansion to include reminders about pre-appointment procedures to be performed has enhanced the value of the practice.[86] The American Cancer Society's "Tell a Friend" program is based on the importance of reminder prompts.[87] In the program, volunteers provide lists of ten women they will contact over a six-month period to encourage them to have mammograms. After six months, the women who were telephoned by a friend were significantly more likely to have had a mammogram since the start of the intervention period than women who were not contacted. The strategy was equally effective for black and white women, with even better results among women with low-to-moderate income.

We may also procrastinate because we're faced with too much information or information comprised of many parts. There's evidence to suggest that we don't always integrate multiple pieces of information about health and behavior to protect our health accurately. For example, in one study of 395 English-speaking adults waiting to see primary care providers in three different cities in the US – one in the north, one in the middle of the nation, and one in the south – patients reviewed actual prescription pill bottle containers with labels[88] and then answered the interviewer's question, "How would you take this medicine?" Three internists rated the participants' responses for accuracy in terms of how much should be taken, how often it should be taken, and for how long the medication was to be taken. Dosage relating to a prescription for pills was inaccurately reported by 28 percent of the participants who reported that the dose was one tablet each day for seven days instead of one tablet by mouth twice daily for seven days. Some of the labels included the instructions, "Take two tablets by mouth twice daily." The patients who had these labels were asked "Show me how many pills you would take of this medicine in one day." The correct response, four, was coded while other responses were incorrect. One third of the participants who were able to state that the instruction said take two tablets by mouth twice daily could *not* demonstrate the correct total number of pills to take each day.

It's not just a matter of having reminder prompts. Sometimes we procrastinate because we never really understood what it was that we were supposed to do in the first place. Hundreds of patients in medical research across the past two decades have been unable to identify the health problem diagnosed by their doctors and what they were supposed to do. This has generated the recommendation that doctors give problem lists or summary letters to patients to help them identify the key points and reinforce the "how" part of what they can do to manage health problems.[89]

Another reason for procrastinating is the reality that prevention and detection practices are seemingly impossible to follow while we still maintain our work and home schedules. Commercial fishermen, truck drivers, farmers and ranchers all have high rates of fatalities associated with their occupations. In such cases, efforts to adapt to risk rather than avoid risk may increase their ability to work and still be safe.[90] Care must be taken not to create new health risks in trying to reduce risks on the job. Pesticide protection in extreme Southern US climates, where heat and humidity make the use of impermeable rubber suits unbearable, contributes to heat stroke due to dehydration. The filtration system in the mask designed to be worn by miners often becomes clogged, leading miners to ignore their use in order to be able to breathe and then contributing to a range of health harms.[91] In these cases, it may be a matter of communicating to employers how and why we cannot follow safety recommendations, a step in the direction of working toward improved recommendations. We may not procrastinate, however, but rather believe that our health is in God's hands and act based on our religious faith and spirituality. This, too, can be a response to the question, "What are my risk factors?"

What God Has To Do with It

Consider how the ways your faith defines rewards and punishments may link to health.

Our spiritual identities and religious faith, or lack thereof, are key in our everyday lives and living. Morals and ethics, personal responsibility – our sense of these fundamental notions emerges in faith discussions and forms our own sense of our spiritual being. This can connect to our health in many ways. It guides our decisions about whether to participate in medical research[92] and our views about what research should be conducted in the first place.[93]

Some of us report that we attend religious services, read religious materials, and pray daily. This contributes to personalizing a relationship with God and forming expectations that God will foretell future health events through prophesies and dreams.[94] If through our religious faith, we believe that we're being held personally responsible for our poor health, the tendency may be to face the "punishment" with as much grace and dignity as we can muster. On the other hand, if through religious faith, we believe that our life is the supreme gift, then we may regard our diagnosis as a "wake-up call" aimed at getting back on the right path to honor our gift.

Members of some religious faith communities tell culturally common stories to reinforce belief in the power of prayer to heal, with retelling about someone's dire medical diagnosis disappearing overnight due to God's power. Some stories reveal the expressed concern that once one seeks God's intervention, seeking help from the formal health care system is an expression of doubt that God will or can act on your behalf. Others may tell stories about how God led a family to find a particular doctor who was possibly the only human who could contribute to a positive health outcome. In both cases, religious faith and spiritual identities are guiding health attitudes and practices. In the former, however, the outcome may lead to worse health outcomes, while the latter may lead to better health outcomes.

In tandem with these realities, our views about the role of science and religion in health and health care emerge. All of these guide how we communicate about health and how we respond to communication about health.[95] Religious faith may be used to justify effort or excuses, depending upon your point of reference, for actions that range from choices about family planning[96] to alcohol and other drug use.[97] Islamic teachings, for example, prohibit use of alcohol and tobacco,[98] with both behaviors having significant negative health effects. An increasing number of churches offer programs that range from fitness and nutrition to depression and marital counseling, as well as substance abuse prevention, with these religious institutions forming an identity around these services. "Caring" and "outreach" are among the labels relating to these religious sites which may house food banks, clothing centers, and other basic requirements for human survival.

Religious faith and spirituality are used to frame the role of religion and spirituality in science, and the role of science in religion and spirituality. The choices function as a harbinger for health literacy, the skills associated with the ability to use health information to promote well-being. This is true for the public but also for our medical professionals, and the influence is bi-directional. Not only are far-reaching decisions made that relate to education and science, but, as illustrated by a growing number of medical schools in the US that offer courses in religion and spirituality,[99] effects will be felt relating to education and religion. There is a tendency, sometimes seemingly unintended but other times apparently quite strategic, to pit science against religion and spirituality in discourse associated with frontiers of discovery around disease and medicine. In doing so, phrases such as "playing God"[100] are used. In these situations, the debate may suddenly turn toward consideration of humans' audacity to enter into a realm reserved for a Higher Power's authority, limiting discussion.[101] Too often, we put our health at risk because we don't recognize an implicit idea being expressed – that belief in God's role for our health and well-being denies belief in science and scientific explanations. Such reductionism has been challenged in the past. The science of religion often asserts that subscribers should view the two as complementary rather than mutually exclusive.

Summing It Up . . .

So much talk about health seems to be aimed at taking the fun out of life. It can be so worrisome, so fearful, so anxiety provoking. Many times, that's because what's rewarding or punishing to us besides good health or bad health will be affected by following the advice. Or following the advice can be so downright dull and boring, time-consuming and difficult, or conflict with our religious faith and values. What is rewarding versus punishing often links back to our views of spirituality and religion. We may feel guilty, ashamed, or fearful when we don't act in ways that reflect our religious faith. We may feel happy, hopeful, or cheerful when we do act in ways that align with faith-based beliefs. Our religious faith also affects our views about personal autonomy in decisions about health and shapes how we allocate our personal time and other resources for health and health care. Unfortunately, our response when all these things don't align with each other is to put off doing what we know we should be doing to protect our health.

We respond to talk about health with our overall identities and many times resist things which seem to be at odds with how we see ourselves. If money is rewarding to us, for example, a message that connects a health practice, such as "quit smoking" or "eat less," to monetary savings should be remembered and acted on to gain the reward. But if the message implies that we're "frugal" when our own identity is aligned with being "generous," then our response may be to just be annoyed. We also respond to talk about health that seems linked to rewards or punishments based on what it says about who's responsible for our health. If a message makes us feel that we're responsible for our health and personal obligation fits within our cultural mindset, it's likely to be remembered and acted on. But if a message makes us feel personally responsible for our health, and we have a more collectivist approach to living, based on family and community being more important than self, the content's unlikely to even gain our attention.

We can go our whole lives without putting our finger on the pulse of why we do what we do. But if we're willing to take a closer look at some of the feelings and experiences we find to be most rewarding and punishing, the insights will give us some measure of understanding, not only for behaviors with health outcomes, but other decisions as well. Recognizing what increases our feelings of happiness, pleasure, and excitement may guide us toward new ways to understand our poor health choices. In turn, a new way of approaching those same situations in the future might be imagined. We may have many good reasons, or excuses, for "putting it off," but they all support the reality that procrastination is a choice. If it's based on not understanding, we have to ask. If it's based on a lack of confidence in our abilities, we have to get help to build new skills. We may feel guilty, ashamed, or fearful when we don't act in ways that reflect what we know we should do. We may feel happy, hopeful, or cheerful when we do act in ways that protect our health. As a result, we may put more effort into being healthy. From both personal and societal perspectives, we can use these insights to guide new answers to the question, "Why don't we get 'care'?"

4

Why Don't We Get "Care"?

In 1997, my future daughter-in-law served in Bosnia as a member of the Army National Guard. She was a journalist writing for the weekly newspaper, *Talon*, funded by the US Army. Beth joined the Guard after high school to help support her college education. After the usual rigors of boot camp and while still juggling her college coursework, her unit was called to serve. And so she became a soldier of Task Force Eagle in Bosnia-Herzegovina, serving at Camp Bedrock. Yes, that's right. Just like the Flintstones, for those of you who remember the cartoon show. They called it Camp Bedrock because it was on the top of a hill in a strip-mined coal mine. Mining continued around the area even as she served her tour of duty. She and my son carried on a long-distance relationship during that time, which included her sharing copies of the *Talon* with me. Through reading the stories there, I learned about all the dimensions of the US involvement and specifically what soldiers at Camp Bedrock were doing beyond the images in the evening news: organizing donations of books to the Bosnian library; teaching Tae-Kwon-Do to locals; helping injured children from the local community with the aid of Army emergency medical staff; seeking deadly mines to destroy them before they injured residents.

Over the months of her duty. Beth sent some pictures like the one in Figure 4.1 to give us a sense of life in Camp Bedrock. We saw her sleeping quarters. She and another woman shared a tent with three men. They used plywood dividers between them and the guys in their unit, with a blanket draped over a bungee cord for a door. She says, "Not a bad bunking experience." It was winter and they used portable heaters in the tent if someone was awake. They turned the heaters off at night to avoid carbon monoxide poisoning or burning the tent down, and the water

Figure 4.1 The author's daughter-in-law pictured during her tour of duty in the Army National Guard while serving in Bosnia.

bottles froze. It was about the length of a football field to the bathrooms, a trip she didn't relish making, especially at night. So she probably went there less often than she might have if they were closer and less often than is healthy. One night, she woke up in horrible pain, doubled over, and barely made it to the bathrooms. She was unarmed, which she worried about because they were supposed to carry their weapon everywhere, but in too much pain to take the time to retrieve it before going. She felt some better after the bathroom but once back in her tent, sat on her cot suffering until sick call, which happened every morning.

Her camp had a doctor and some nurses in a medical trailer. The doctors saw soldiers in the order the nurses placed them based on triage conducted in a big tent. If the camp doctor could take care of a soldier, he did. Otherwise, he gave permission for the soldier to go to a military hospital run by a reserve medical unit, not the National Guard. It was on a Swedish base and reached by a long bus ride. When the doctor examined Beth, he said she had an infection but he also felt a mass. He gave her some meds for the infection and said that if she kept having pain, she needed to come back. They would send her to Germany for more tests. She never went back. Her parents were, as she says today, "totally freaked." But she didn't want to be sent to Germany because she didn't want her fellow soldiers to think she was trying to "get out of theater," the hazardous duty zone they were in. The infection cleared up, but she spent the rest of deployment worried about the mass.

Once Beth was back in the US, other military doctors also felt the mass. But it wasn't until she completed her tour of duty and went home from deployment that she had an ultrasound at the VA hospital. They didn't find anything on the ultrasound, yet she felt certain that there was something, since two doctors had told her they felt something was there. Scared, she went to her civilian doctor who referred her to her mother's gynecologist. Another ultrasound was performed, and that technician had no trouble seeing that all of her organs were pulled to one side. They suspected endometriosis as the diagnosis. She was scheduled for surgery within two weeks and they found she had Stage 4 endometriosis. Endometriosis is a condition in which the endometrial tissue lining the inside of the uterus grows outside the uterus and attaches to other organs, including ovaries and fallopian tubes. Stage 4 means that it was extensive. After surgery to remove the overgrown tissue, the surgeon told her that he thought what the other doctors felt was actually her colon. Since the endometriosis was so bad and had pulled all her organs to the left, when her colon was full it felt like a mass. Beth's experience turned out fine, as she got care that preserved her fertility. But her path along the way reveals many of the reasons that we don't get care. Sometimes we don't have access either due to our inability to afford care or its lack of availability to us where we're located. But even when we have access, we may not get care because our doctor didn't recommend it, one answer to the question, "Why don't we get care?"

Our Doctors Didn't Recommend It

Doctors benefit from memory prompts, too.

How often have you gone to a doctor's appointment expecting a particular diagnosis or treatment recommendation, but it didn't happen? As

Beth's experience illustrates, our doctors don't always recommend that we get care even when we or others might think that they should. While the doctor told Beth to come back if she continued to experience pain, he didn't tell her to come back even if the pain went away, so that they could deal with "the mass" he felt in her abdomen. She eventually ended up with a medical discharge because she couldn't perform her duties.

Why don't doctors recommend care when we might think that they should? Sometimes, it's as simple as the fact that therapies simply aren't available. We may have heard a news report about research that shows a promising new drug to prevent the pain associated with a chronic condition such as arthritis, or a report about the discovery of a gene linked to heart disease. But that doesn't mean that the drug's available yet for standard care or that there's a genetic test for a gene talked about in the report. Doctors may not tell us about these options being *un*available unless we ask about them. Otherwise, it would be an odd conversation going something like this. The doctor would say, "You may have heard about research linking genes to heart disease. No? Well never mind," leaving you to wonder, "What was that about?" On the other hand, if you say, "Yes," then your doctor's left to say, "OK. Well, we can't test you for the genes because there aren't any tests available yet." To which you think, "Why'd you bring it up then?" Or the doctor might say, "We could test you for the genes, but there isn't any new therapy besides what we're already doing. So just continue to exercise, watch your weight, and take the medication that seems to be helping lower your cholesterol levels." To which you might think, "OK . . ."

Sometimes, doctors may not recommend a particular type of care because it's still in an experimental clinical trial phase.[102] Doctors often say that they lack time to explain clinical trials to patients. Some say that participating would be too much burden on particular patients, requiring them to travel great distances or find child care. And sometimes doctors say the intensive and often intrusive protocol associated with an experimental therapy is too much for some patients. Doctors also worry that proposing a clinical trial will harm their relationship with patients. And they observe that just talking about trials with patients is an indirect way of telling them that their condition has no known effective treatment.[103]

Doctors may not recommend some types of care because they don't look at our health status the same way that we do. Something that may seem like a big deal to us and in need of costly intervention may seem quite manageable to them with simple and inexpensive therapies such as taking an aspirin a day. Or our diagnosis may be "normal" based on our age or other characteristics. I had a doctor tell me that very thing, for example, regarding the development of arthritis in my hip area at about the age of 30. If no one says as much, however, we may feel dissatisfied with what seems like dismissal of our complaint.

Doctors can't recommend some types of care because they're employees who must operate within the constraints of the organizations they work for.[104] There are limits on their time and other resources based on where and for whom they work. Some hospital services have been eliminated in response to advice to "build up your winners, weed out your losers." As a result, for example, inpatient psychiatric units which had low occupancy and lost money have been closed, limiting options for doctors to recommend to patients. There have also been reductions in staffing in many health care organizations, which reduces support for doctors in their care of patients. Doctors recommend some hospitals for care rather than others because hospitals develop contracts with individual doctors and groups to provide exclusive coverage for various services. Doctors who aren't members of medical staff cannot get access to the hospital. This shift is intended to produce cost-savings and higher-quality patient care as it standardizes specialized procedures or services.

Doctors also forget to bring up some issues with us even when they've raised them in the past or promised to discuss them at a future appointment. Among all the issues that may be in our chart, they select the ones we make most relevant by our statements of why we have an appointment that day. So, not surprisingly, doctors benefit from cues to assist in prompting them to discuss some things with us as patients. Chart reminders, for example, have been found to increase the likelihood that doctors will talk about prevention guidelines.[105] And we can prompt our doctor to talk about something they've mentioned in the past to us if we're wondering how they think we're doing or how important it is to our health.

Finally, even when our doctors *do* make recommendations to us, we sometimes don't understand, don't remember, or choose not to follow them. One time when I was observing doctors and patients interacting, a patient with canker sores was told by her doctor to be careful not to swallow the prescribed medication because it "numbs like Novocain."

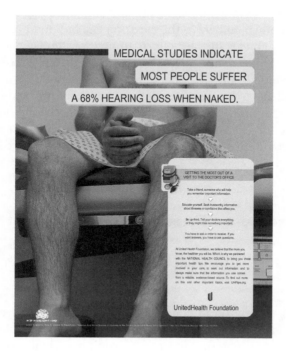

Figure 4.2   The medical exam may impair our hearing and contribute to a lack of understanding. Source: United Health Foundation. Reproduced by permission.

In a follow-up interview, the patient said that she didn't fill her prescription because she didn't want to feel "like I'd been to the dentist." The patient chose not to follow her doctor's advice mostly because of how she interpreted the metaphor used to explain the prescribed medication. Cultural practices contribute to whether we understand, remember, or follow guidelines as well. This sometimes limits the care we get. The meaning of silence, for example, affects how we respond to a doctor's recommendations. In some cultures, silence is a sign of respect. However, in a medical appointment, a patient's silence signals implicit agreement or understanding.[106] As suggested by Figure 4.2, sometimes we literally don't hear a doctor's recommendation. A medical exam may increase our physiological arousal and interfere with hearing ability. We all know that feeling of our heart racing or beating so loudly that we can't think, and we can't hear either.

In making recommendations, doctors recognize the importance of including family members in the care process, but don't always do it.[107] They face challenges in their efforts to involve families, because some family members demand more access to doctors than is possible in their schedules. Some family members challenge the doctors' medical decisions.[108] Still, doctors often do collaborate with family members, asking them to gather important information or report symptoms that the patient may forget. This is just part of the vital role that the support of family and friends plays in whether we get health care in a formal system.

Family or Friends Don't Support It

Family and friends may have no more resources to support health than you do.

Do you ever look around yourself and wonder how you can possibly even think about going to the doctor? No time. No money. No way. While Beth's situation is one that most of us won't experience, isolation from family is a common experience. We live in places where we find work or schooling, or where we want to live, and it may be a far distance from family. We form friendships based on work, other interests, and where we live. We're sometimes more concerned about what our friends think about us than we are about acting on health advice. We don't want our co-workers to think we're shirking our responsibilities on the job.

Family and friends' support, or lack of support, many times predicts whether we get care from formal health systems or not. They also affect what we expect when we see a doctor and our judgments of the doctor's expertise and trustworthiness.[109] Family members and friends can support us in getting care by recommending that we make appointments with doctors. When they do, we're more likely to follow through.[110] So when they say they expect us to keep medical appointments, take medication to control high blood pressure, get a mammogram, or other health promoting behaviors, they're likely to be there to help us follow through. Their support is more likely to predict that we get care than our exposure to TV, radio, newspapers, or magazines talking about healthy habits.[111]

Since family is so important, why wouldn't they make sure we do what we need to do to protect our health? Family members may not advise us to do things to protect our health because they don't have the resources to support our efforts. The cost of care can be particularly problematic. When one family member is uninsured and has an accident, a hospital stay, or some other form of costly treatment, the bills affect the economic stability for the *entire* family.[112] Some estimate that in the US, the need to cover the expenses of health care is the cause for about 25 percent of families being unable to pay rent or mortgage. But even in the Netherlands where they have universal access to high-quality care, one study of 315 patients with early stage breast or colorectal cancers found that a partner's opinion was given more weight among patients who had no paid employment compared to those who had paid employment.[113]

Family and friends can't support what they don't know. Sometimes, we may fear that someone we hope will support us won't, letting us down and not behaving as "true friends." So we just don't risk it by telling them about our health. How families talk every day about matters besides health sets our expectations in these matters. In some families, there are more questions, more advice giving, and more interpretation. In other families, there's more quiet reflection, together with confirmation of each other, and acknowledgment of each other.[114] In reality, however, our family or friends don't recommend that we get care or support our efforts to seek "care" from medical sites because they frequently are the ones who provide our care.

We Use Support Networks

Recognize the care we get from mutual aid and natural support networks.

When you think about your health, who's the first person you tell your symptoms to or what's the first source of information you want when deciding what to do? Most of us give the same answers. Our family. Our friends. Perhaps people we work with. Maybe someone in our church, synagogue, or mosque. Quite simply, our first lessons about how to care for our health don't come from doctors. We develop habits based on what our family does. The diet we eat. Our views of nutrition. Our beliefs about illness causation, about sexuality, and about life and death form in families, which are a natural support system for health.

In my own family, one of my cousins was never physically present at the family reunion picnics held on the beach each summer in northern Michigan. He was just a bit older than me and had congenital muscular dystrophy. He never grew strong enough to eat more than baby cereal and struggled to swallow that. My aunt kept him at home for as long as she possibly could manage to lift him from his crib. She followed the advice of doctors and nurses who suggested ways to care for him. He was always present when we visited his home, always cared for, and always loved. We all counted him as an important part of the family, not hiding him away, no shame, and with hope for a better tomorrow. He lived into his teens, and as my aunt got older and my cousin got bigger, maturing into a large infant-looking human without muscle control in his limbs and still struggling to swallow every bite ladled into his mouth, he eventually had to have institutional care. He didn't live very much longer after that, and family members said that without all the family's love, it just didn't much matter to him whether he lived on.

Besides our family, we also often receive a great deal of care from lay health care providers or workers. Lay health care is an expression used to refer to care we get from people who aren't certified health care professionals but have been trained in some way to promote health.[115] They may be trained to teach parents how to talk about sex to their teenagers, for example, or to assist families in understanding the care needed for a dying family member. They may teach female migrant farmworkers how to conduct breast self exams and why it's important to do so. They might even be trained to give shots in a situation where inoculations for large numbers of people are needed and there aren't sufficient certified caregivers to do it.

The availability and use of sources of lay health care have increased in response to a number of realities of the end of the twentieth century that have continued into the twenty-first century. Formal medical systems may recognize the need to provide more culturally sensitive care but be unable to employ doctors who speak the primary language of some patients or understand their health beliefs and practices. Culture guides the development of language, attitudes, values, behaviors, relationships, and the structure of social organizations including political, religious, and legal.[116] These all have connections to how we view communicating about health and the control we have over our health. Culture many times guides the beliefs families have and the decisions they make about whether to use formal health care. These decisions, in turn, relate to whether the medical system integrates cultural practices, such as food choices in the hospital and prayer rituals, into formal care. Some primetime medical dramas have portrayed the importance of these issues for decisions about whether to get medical care. These include episodes, for example, where families bring more indigenous foods into the hospital so the patient can eat what he or she is used to eating.

Formal health care systems have several paths they pursue relating to the cultural backgrounds of populations that they serve.[117] They can make efforts to understand different cultural perspectives and accommodate as many as feasible, preserve practices found to be beneficial, or attempt to revise cultural practices found to be harmful to health. For example, even just allowing family members to be present has been hard to get approved in many medical settings. Sometimes, it's a practical matter, such as the size of a waiting or examination room which limits accommodation, or operating hours which restrict working families' ability to come to the clinic. An inability to accommodate these needs contributes to reliance on lay health providers. On the other hand, Native American indigenous healers use herbal medicines, some of which have been the origin of modern drugs based on botanicals. Knowing about these can promote doctors' abilities to preserve these practices and even integrate them into care for all patients. Sometimes, however, accommodation or preservation isn't possible. Some Hispanic, Arabic, South Asian, and Chinese groups, for example, use lead in folk medicine, and lead-glazed pottery for cooking. These practices may contribute to lead poisoning, especially among children. Efforts to reduce exposure to lead may require the formal health care system to revise strongly held beliefs and practices linked to folk medicine or cooking.

Sometimes, indigenous healers – such as *curanderos* who practice *curanderismo*, emphasizing health as mind, body, and spirit – are the only care available because of a lack of geographic or financial access to formal public or private health services. Research has shown, however, that users are not limited to low-income clients. Middle-class users often access indigenous systems of care or use the knowledge derived from them. For example, I'd never even heard of using aloe for burns until I married and was united into a family with pioneering roots. During those years of living in Arizona and participating in ranching activities on my husband's family ranch, more than once I observed someone bend and slice a part of a cactus and apply it to a burn or other wound. Now, I always have a bottle of 100 percent aloe chilled in my refrigerator for the moments when, despite our best efforts, someone ends up with a sunburn. So I am a benefactor of this indigenous knowledge. I have not, however, experienced indigenous healing.

Faith-based organizations and other community groups frequently provide support for health and well-being outside formal health care systems. Mutual aid networks emphasize the value of social support including information, tangible resources, and emotional support. This in turn forms a network of mutual obligations. The interdependency contributes to reciprocity of aid, responses to problems as experienced, flexibility to respond to changing needs, and active participation – which is viewed as mandatory. Millions of members in tens of thousands of groups emphasize the role that these self-help groups have as advocates and even as liaisons to complement professional health services. One of the first graduate students I advised, Tina Harris, who is now a Professor at the University of Georgia, shares her story in Table 4.1 about her brother, pictured as a toddler in Figure 4.2, and how church, family, and faith came together to support her brother's healing.

Even when our doctor has recommended care for us or referred us for care to another medical professional, our family and friends support it, and our other support systems do too, it isn't always the case that we will follow through. Or, if we do, something happens at those appointments where it doesn't end up working out the way it was intended. This may happen because we communicate about health to manage impressions – our own, those of our support systems, and even those of the doctors that we go to for care.

We're Managing Impressions

Realize that communicating to save face for self, or others, may lead to worse physical *and* mental health.

How many times do we do something that relates to our health that we wish we could take back? Sometimes, it happens quite unintentionally,

Figure 4.3 The brother of one of the author's friends, as a baby and a young child, pictured with tracheotomy tube before his healing by faith.

as when you try that new skin product and it makes you break out in a rash right before you have an important public event. Sometimes, it happens with some intention, as you think what you're doing will help your health but it doesn't work out that way. My dad and I are particularly susceptible to poison ivy. He had a bad breakout that was causing fits of itching. He'd used all the usual things and was getting no relief. He was in the laundry room and picked up the bleach bottle, thinking that maybe that would "clean" it up and stop the itching. He poured it over his arm, which was in that blistering and oozing phase. The bleach had barely touched him before he wished he could take it back. One of my sisters is a nurse and she begged him during the days that followed to go to the doctor but he wouldn't. He knew he'd done something "stupid" and didn't want to face telling the doctor about it. Luckily, he didn't end up losing his arm over his refusal to get care, but there were some tense days while he healed.

Situations like my dad's are more common than most of us care to admit. And while there are many times when we're aware that we're trying to manage our impression, communicating about health may not be one of them. We think about job interviews and plan what to say in order to manage our impressions. But we may not be as strategic when it comes to talking about our health. Whether we make as much effort to plan for these conversations or not, it's likely that we present ourselves in ways that support our sense of self and identity. This plays out in two primary ways.[118] We act in ways that we believe will make others be more

Table 4.1 One of the author's friends describes her family's faith healing experience.

I was born into a family of faith who believed that God was (and is) in control in every situation. This belief was truly tested in 1981 when my younger brother Ken was 11 months old and had difficulty breathing. His breathing was so labored that my mother became seriously concerned and took him to the emergency room at the local hospital. Dad was out of town on business. Upon their arrival at the ER, Mom spoke with the physician on duty. After examining Ken and giving him a breathing treatment, the doctor concluded he would be fine and my mother could take Ken home, even though he wasn't getting any better. My mother prayed that the doctors would find out what was wrong with her baby boy. But Ken wasn't getting better. In fact, he was getting progressively worse and Mom knew that something more serious was wrong. Mom requested that the emergency room physician contact Ken's pediatrician, who finally arrived and concluded that Ken did in fact need hospitalization for further diagnosis.

Throughout this trying time, Mom and Dad prayed and solicited the prayers of the church community, family and friends, seeking God to heal their son. After a series of tests and consulting with specialists, it was determined that he had viral croup, a viral infection of the voice box and windpipe that severely narrows the windpipe and cuts off breathing. He was not responding to the treatment and was not improving. Ken was at this hospital for two weeks. After much prayer, and without the approval of the attending physicians, Mom and Dad were led to transfer him to Egleston Children's Hospital. Upon their arrival at Egleston, Ken was rushed to the Intensive Care unit and emergency surgery was performed. A tracheotomy tube was inserted in his throat to help him breathe. This trip to the emergency room turned into a 31-day journey before Ken would return home. He celebrated his first birthday in the hospital.

For the next $3^{1}/_{2}$ *years*, there were repeated visits to doctors office and ER for infections and colds. Each visit to the doctor in hopes of having the tracheotomy removed was disappointing. Eventually a doctor who was a missionary, a man of faith, and experienced with severe respiratory ailments in children was assigned to Ken's case. He stood in faith with my parents that Ken could be healed through medical intervention or surgery where cartilage would be taken from Ken's rib to build him a windpipe. On the day of Ken's surgery, they went in to do the procedure and the doctor was amazed! Ken did not need the surgery – his windpipe had been miraculously healed! He was wheeled back to his room, observed for 48 hours, and released. Today, Ken is a healthy young man, with no signs of breathing problems! He is a mental health clinician, a student affairs counselor at Georgia Perimeter College, and the Director of Music at New Generation Christian Fellowship Church, where our mother is pastor. More importantly, Ken *sings* praises to God *every* Sunday – a true miracle.
Dr Tina Harris, University of Georgia

likely to like us. And we act in ways that we think will limit the restrictions others place on our freedom to behave as we want to behave. It's pretty easy to imagine how that affects what we're willing to disclose to our doctors. But there are some times when it's more likely to happen. For example, when we don't understand a disease process, we have problems talking about it. So why don't we just tell the doctor we don't understand? Perhaps because it seems like we should understand and we don't want to seem uninformed or just downright stupid. But the result may be that we don't give the doctor an important detail about our health.

It's not only patients who don't understand. Sometimes, doctors don't understand, and we may be a cause of their lack of understanding. Some of us tend to avoid direct statements of "no." If patients don't tell doctors, "No, I can't follow that advice," they may end up not getting care because doctors think patients have agreed with and followed a recommended therapy. As discussed in Chapter 2, we often rely on stories to understand health and health care. A second challenge to doctors' understanding and providing us with the best care is our use of *stories* to tell doctors about our experiences. We may tell a story when the doctor asks how we are doing to make our behavior, which led to our poor health, seem to make more sense and make us more likable. A patient's story, which may be intended to communicate how much pain is being experienced or how disruptive poor health is, may actually describe the inability to perform family and work roles, so a doctor may not "hear" the symptom. Sometimes, doctors do recognize patients' reluctance to report symptoms in efforts to manage their own or family members' symptoms. This has been observed in pediatric primary care settings where parents identified emotional and developmental problems of their children on a checklist, but only raised about 40 percent of the issues with their doctors.[119] The doctors nonetheless recognized many of the problems.

Even when we do understand the disease process, telling others about our feelings and fears is still very difficult. When faced with a serious diagnosis, we often don't know how to communicate about it, what questions to ask, including opinions about prognosis, with some research revealing that we don't ask for more information because we're trying to manage our impression.[120] When we don't talk about these issues and our possible concerns, not surprisingly, it often leads to delay in getting treatment, but also has been found to intensify the intrusive thoughts associated with thinking about the diagnosis, which may contribute to worse physical and mental health. While we don't often think about managing our impression in terms of communicating about health, it is rather easy to see how it gets into the mix of things.

Doctors, public health messages, and advertisements unintentionally put us in a position of withholding information about ourselves to present an image that matches our identity and self-concept. Men, for example, preserve a version of masculine identity associated with being strong by withdrawing from conversations about health.[121] We may have engaged in practices in the past that are now known to be harmful to our health. While some of these, such as exposures to asbestos, seemingly have no negative implications for self-presentation purposes, others – such as smoking – may seem irrelevant if they happened many years ago. But, as noted in Chapter 1, medical research evolves. Science changes. Some research suggests that smoking, even in a far distant past, if combined with some other exposures, such as asbestos, may contribute to lung cancer many years later. So doctors may ask us about our jobs and possible exposures to asbestos. And while we may not quite understand the nature of the puzzle being pieced together to represent illness and disease causation, some questions from our doctors are less face-threatening than others.

We manage our impressions relating to health with our partners, family, and friends as well. We limit talk about health with them because we don't want to be perceived as needy, again managing our impressions. We also don't want to limit their freedoms to behave without the constraints our health status might impose on them. For example, talking about health histories in families can be difficult and is often avoided. These conversations may arouse fear without suggesting how to manage the risk related to our family history. So we frequently just avoid them, rarely or never talking about medical histories in our families.[122]

Age makes a difference in the likelihood of our disclosing, being heard when we disclose, and receiving appropriate care in some cases. With an aging population worldwide, it's important to recognize that if we try to manage our impressions by avoiding disclosure of our pain experiences, they're unlikely to be addressed by our doctors. As discussed in Chapter 2, pain isn't "normal" but has sometimes been normalized as part of aging. So, doctors often don't ask elderly patients about it and when confronted with statements about pain, they may even dismiss them.

The older we get, the more we may have to prod our doctors to give us information about health. Doctors sometimes may limit the amount of information they give to an elderly patient, believing that as the amount given increases, recall decreases. This is, however, a reality for all of us and shouldn't be used as an excuse not to offer test results and other information to elderly patients. Disclosure, in other words, is a two-way street, and managing impressions based on stereotypes contributes to poor health outcomes.

There are also structural barriers to our willingness to disclose as we strive to manage our impression. Some of these relate to being asked to reveal sensitive information in a setting where others are present. This may be our own family member or members, or even a partner or friend who doesn't know something about our past behavior or our present feelings. The doctor is in a challenging situation in this case, as allowing us to have these people present has been found to enhance the likelihood that we will follow through with recommendations as previously discussed. And as already discussed, in some clinics, having these additional people present has been a hard-fought battle to make it happen. So the idea that their presence may pose face threats to patients is a hurdle that we must navigate together with our doctors if it poses a barrier to our care.

Beyond those whom we bring with us into the examining room, modern medicine is often conducted by a team. This occurs both because there are doctors in training and because we break the body into so many parts that a doctor may need to be present to talk about our health in relation to a number of areas, all of which are affecting our well-being. But asking us to reveal sensitive information in front of a group of people increases the likelihood that we won't end up getting the best care because we won't end up disclosing everything that we might have under different circumstances. An explanation for why so many caregivers are present may ease discomfort with the situation. Additionally, specific statements about how an organization is safeguarding medical information may increase our disclosure levels, and the subsequent accuracy of diagnosis as well as treatment. Doctors should assess their requests for sensitive information and avoid asking if it isn't really necessary. Otherwise, our temptation to avoid telling may be supported by our tendency to think that not telling doesn't really matter, because we're "doomed" anyway, or "everything will be all right."

We're too Optimistic or Fatalistic

Know that *when* it gets done often predicts health outcomes, good or bad.

Why do we do it? We think to ourselves, "It's just a bad cold," or "I'll give the pain one more day to go away," or "It's probably just hemorrhoids." Beth worried about the mass in her abdomen, but she didn't get care until she was back in the US. She was worried but optimistic that since the infection was better, she'd be OK. It turns out that this is a common reason that we don't get formal health "care" – our tendency to believe that everything will be fine. Or, at the other extreme, an attitude that reflects something like, "If it's our time, it's our time." We sometimes feel the latter as we recognize our symptoms to be ones that seem to be related to very serious diagnoses. But, if we can't afford to be told that we're seriously ill or can't afford to be hospitalized, we don't even take the step of getting a diagnosis. It all starts to intermingle as worry about the economic and social reality of our lives keeps us from telling our family and friends. They can't support us in making the appointment to get checked because we don't tell them we have a problem. We don't tell them we have a problem because we know they can't afford it and neither can we. In female-led households, there is the additional reality of diminished extended family networks. There's the inability to miss work *and* the inability to leave children unattended to obtain health care. Thus, many mothers literally can't "afford" to be sick, as the costs become too great to the family overall. So they're left with being optimistic that things will work out.

We have general tendencies to believe we're more likely to experience positive outcomes when faced with threats to our well-being than others who experience the same event. Somehow, we just manage to see ourselves as less likely to be vulnerable to a health risk or to see the risk as less severe for us than it's depicted. One way we allow ourselves to do this in the face of knowing about a risk is through an "othering process."[123] We identify a group that doesn't include us and label them as the ones who are at risk for those bad things to happen. This is used to support our decision not to seek care. We take family history into account, for example, in coming up with our assessments. So if we don't have a family history of the health risk being considered, or don't know about it at least, those who do become the "others." "That" group at risk. So even though we may know the signs of such diseases as diabetes, hypertension, cancer, arthritis, or heart attacks, if no one in our family has them, we're more likely to be optimistic that we won't be affected.[124] So we don't seek care.

Our optimism increases with perceived control.[125] The more we think we have control over the outcomes of our actions, the less we are bothered by the thought of not acting promptly. So we may experience some symptoms, including pain or shortness of breath, but if we can keep on working, they must not be that bad. If they begin to interfere with our work, we reason, then we'll get care. Perhaps this is the explanation for the numbers of men and women who die at their desks from heart attacks each year. Research that has examined optimistic bias in heavy smokers found that their estimates of the likelihood that they would live to be at least 75 years old were twice what actuarial studies projected life expectancy to be.[126] Many of us have known a smoker who proclaimed that his grandfather lived to be 103 years old and smoked three packs of cigarettes each day. While such an individual may acknowledge that smoking relates to lung cancer, and that heredity relates to lung cancer, they may be optimistically biased in assessing their personal risk. They have both an absence of lung cancer in the family and the presence of the grandfather who smoked heavily and lived a long life. At the other extreme, feeding into our fatalism and failure to get care, if we believe that a health problem or cause of death is influenced by heredity, we're more likely to have fatalistic views about our health and believe that we have no control over the problem.[127]

How will our optimistic or fatalistic views relate to our responses to messages about genes and health? Single gene disorders in which disease is caused by defects in one particular gene, such as cystic fibrosis or sickle cell disease, will be far outnumbered by the multiple genes that science is now linking to common disorders such as heart disease, cancer, and diabetes. Will messages about these links identify genes as the primary relevant contributor to an individual's characteristics and life courses? If so, will that lead us to avoid health care or not behave in health-promoting ways? With regard to conclusions associated with environmental influence on disease, we may be somewhat pessimistic about the role of the environment, too.[128] If we maintain a multifaceted view of illness causation, it may help us to recognize these tendencies in ourselves and others, and to avoid unwarranted pessimism or optimism.

Summing It Up . . .

What a cycle of misunderstanding and mistrust swarms around talk about
getting biomedical care in formal health systems. It's true enough that
we sometimes don't get care when we want or need it. But many times
we use other sources, including family and friends, or support systems
in our religious sites and communities. Family and friends are also the
ones who have the best success in getting us to go to the doctor when
we should and to follow the routines and recommendations doctors give
us. That's because, if they recommend it, they're there to support us in
doing it. But they won't always tell us to go, even when they know that
we should, because they, like us, are limited in the time, money, and other
resources they have to put toward health. And in all that talk about health,
there aren't many ideas about how to do more with less when it comes
to getting formal care – how to get more resources when they're needed
– or how to make "going to the doctor" more fun and more rewarding,
less punishing and scary, or even less boring.

Recognizing that we form a vast network of mutual obligations and
support relating to health and care can aid our understanding of why
we do what we do. These support networks shoulder fears and concerns
about our well-being. They feel responsible not only for our care when
we need it, but for roles that we may not be able to fulfill when ill. Oddly
enough, knowing that, we limit our disclosures about health to them
in order to limit their worries and manage our impression and theirs in
our relationships. Too often, this happens without much intention or
awareness. But recognizing that this is a reality is a step in making sense
out of all the talk about health care. Identities form from communication about getting health care, based on the statistics and the stories,
and our sense of what's rewarding and punishing. These get in the
way of getting care. We, after all, want to manage information about
ourselves.

We want to feel that when we seek care, we won't be humiliated
or embarrassed, or find that it keeps us from getting the jobs we want.
We want our doctors to give us the ability to have control over our
thoughts and feelings relating to health. We want to be free to think,
form attitudes, and react within our own value systems. In doing so, we
need to know that our family and friends will still love and care for us.
We want to be free to maintain an identity separate from the medical

setting. So, we go in search of care among others who treat our whole self. We want to determine with whom and under what circumstances we share our thoughts and feelings. And as a result, we sometimes tell no one. So we adopt an optimistic outlook and put off getting care.

We also want to be free to determine when we seek advice. We want to trust that our doctors present various options for care to us. Our concern that they might not contributes to our resistance to seeking care. Our resistance to seeking care, of course, limits what our doctors can recommend to us to promote our well-being. It's sometimes hard to draw the line between when we choose alternative treatments and use indigenous sources of care because we rationally considered the choices and when we're trying to manage our impressions. The truth that we manage interactions to preserve identities also predicts our response to some public health messages and advertisements. It thus becomes important to assess, "Is the 'public good' good for me?" when drawing conclusions about how communicating about health affects us.

5

Is the "Public Good" Good for Me?

My granddaughter's third birthday was coming up and my husband had been on an annual hunting trip with his brothers and my son. The trip finished a couple of days before her birthday, so my husband decided to stay over for the celebration before returning home. I'll never forget the phone call during which he told me about the preschool party. "We had to go to the grocery store and buy cupcakes for it," he said. "What?" I asked in surprise, as our daughter-in-law loves to bake and is super at it. "Yeah. They don't allow anything home-baked to be brought in for the kids to eat. It has to come from the store and to still be in its sealed container." So much for those cupcake containers I'd recently seen on an infomercial that I'd been thinking about as a gift. "How come?" "Health rules," he replied. "All those peanut allergies and such. I guess the preschool can't be too careful." "Wow."

It reminded me of being a parent in my own children's high school athletic booster clubs. The policies and practices aimed at keeping food and drink safe that applied to our groups made the fund-raising sometimes seem almost more bother than it was worth. I remember on occasion thinking, "Why don't we just divide up the profit made from all this effort among the parents who are volunteering and donate the proceeds – it sure would take a lot less time and be a lot less frustrating." But that was only sometimes when my work schedule was too hectic and I needed a reminder to slow it down anyway. The rest of the time, I realized that the community forged among parents participating in the booster clubs was the reward as much and more than raising monies for our kids' activities.

Efforts like the ones connected to my granddaughter's preschool and my children's booster clubs are aimed at protecting the public's health.

Just like when the radio announcer reminds, "Get your flu shot," "Get your mammogram," "Wear sunscreen," "Don't drink and drive," "Get a gun safety trigger lock to save the life of a child." These messages cast a wide net aimed at the population at large and communicate about health as a public good. A public good is something that, by definition, benefits everyone and cannot be withheld from anyone. When I receive a flu vaccine, it's intended to keep me from getting the flu. If I don't get the flu, I also won't spread the virus to anyone with whom I come in contact. So the benefit I reap can't be withheld from some while protecting others. The cost of that benefit isn't any more for everyone than it is just for me.

When health is treated as a public good, the overarching goal is to set priorities that use resources to the greatest good of the greatest number of citizens. Health as a public good thus has a population rather than an individual focus.[129] Population-based approaches depend upon epidemiological data,[130] with epidemiology being the study of disease prevalence. Prevalence is the number of cases which exist in a population at a particular point in time and is often compared between countries to help identify possible causes for disease. Prevalence of heart disease in France, for example, has been compared to Britain, with possible explanations for differences being offered as strategies to reduce risk. Incidence, a second term used in making population comparisons and guiding decisions about how to use resources for the public's good, is the number of *new* cases in a population that occur during a *specific period* of time, usually one year. Incidence of heart disease, for example, has been shown to be on the rise. This has been attributed to higher consumption of animal fats, a practice that began earlier in Britain than France, and earlier in the US than either country.

Our expectations about health and the health care system are often linked to our understanding of prevalence and incidence. While doctors may talk to us about our individual risk for disease and benefit from treatment, we often draw conclusions about our personal risk from communication based on prevalence or incidence in the population. One survey of 2,000 women in the US between the ages of 45 and 64 years, for example, found that more than 60 percent incorrectly believed that mammography reduced the incidence of breast cancer.[131] The opposite may actually be true. If a media campaign saturated television, radio, and even the internet with messages about the importance of getting a mammogram, women might increase their use of this detection practice. This could lead to the identification of more cancers in the year in which exposure to the campaign took place. This might make the incidence look like it has increased when in reality, an accurate assessment of incidence is what has increased. This is important for us to consider when we try to understand the effects of all the talk about health as a public good. This talk reveals when we have no choice but to disclose information about our health status, as well as when some of our personal freedoms may be limited to promote the public's health, when these protections get unevenly distributed, how nonprofit organizations contribute to the greater good of the public, and why civil government's role in the public's health matters. Since the glue, so to speak, that binds all of these matters is the data collected about our health, consideration of when and how that happens is a foundation for starting to sort out the talk about health around health as a public good.

When We Have to "Tell"

If you *want* to be counted, if you truly want to be counted – tell all you can about your health status. In doing so, however, recognize the possible costs.

Who knows *what* about your health status? What lab reports and results based on you go into databases to form knowledge about the public's health? From the moment of our birth in most nations, someone collects information about us that will be used to communicate about health as a public good.[132] Most of us don't give it much thought. It's not like anyone ever really asks us if we want to give the information. Our "telling" in the form of our data is instead required. We give what is called "implied consent" by showing up to get care. It's a process and a practice that begins with newborn screening. When my first grandchild was born in 2003, I was thrilled to be there. I got to hold her just minutes after her birth, as shared in Figure 5.1. And I was there when her parents received the news that she didn't "pass" her newborn hearing test. Not so thrilling. The fact that hearing problems are such a common birth defect has contributed to use of this screening in many places throughout the world. Early diagnosis contributes to the ability to limit the negative effects on learning and social development.

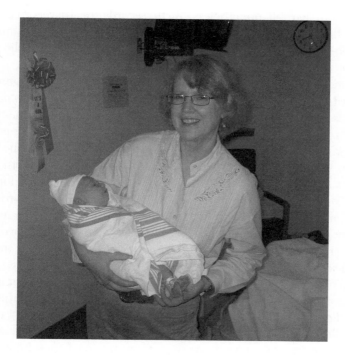

Figure 5.1   The author at the birth of her first grandchild who was delivered by caesarean section and didn't pass the newborn screening test for hearing until retested.

Automated auditory brainstem response test involves putting jelly tab sensors to the head and a computer then receives and records the baby's response to sound. A soft earphone making clicking sounds is used to see if the baby responds. Finding out that she didn't pass was, in fact, a fearful moment that lasted for hours.

The test administrator was good about telling us that it was common for babies delivered by caesarean section not to "pass" the first time. A vaginal delivery often pushes fluids out of a newborn's ears that may remain in the ears of a baby delivered by C-section. When my grand-daughter's test was repeated 24 hours later, she responded normally, a great relief to us all. But also revealing. What we "tell" decision-makers, either implicitly or explicitly, contributes to the evidence base. We tell them often without specific intention or insight to the fact that we're telling. But we tell nonetheless. Birth records, death records, and a whole host of data in between tell them. Who's the "them" in this scenario? The organizations and personnel that make up our public health systems across the world.

Newborn screening programs throughout the world have generally followed the path of implied consent, allowing only religion as possible grounds for not participating.[133] The UK, however, has made great strides in efforts to adopt a policy of "informed consent" for newborn screening, developing a document like the ones we might be asked to sign before having surgery. These forms describe the risks and benefits of a medical procedure. The UK's program to screen for PKU, phenylketonuria – a condition which left untreated can retard brain development – which began in 1969 and continues in the twenty-first century, exemplifies an informed consent approach.[134] A mother receives a pre-screening leaflet in the third trimester of her pregnancy and it is to be discussed at least 24 hours before the baby's screening, prescribed to take place between five and eight days after birth. The leaflet is to be used to decide whether to consent or not. The benefits are outlined in the leaflet, including emphasis on the importance of obtaining care at the earliest moment for any child diagnosed with PKU. Not surprisingly, mothers are nearly unanimous in consenting. And they know what and why the test is being done. Such informed consent for screening is, however, the exception rather than the rule. Partly, concerns about arousing unnecessary anxiety lead to recommendations only to inform parents with affected children about these tests and their meaning. In the process of protecting us from these emotions, we are also denied an opportunity to better understand health and the tests used to establish our status.

Our "telling" at birth is just the beginning. As suggested by the newborn screening programs, our medical lab data are important for guiding public policies. From such data, disease registries form. Disease registries depend upon the collection of data about our health status. Disease registries also depend upon accurate clinical diagnoses. We play a role in this, as elaborated throughout this book. Our ability to talk about our family history, for example, contributes to the accuracy of the evidence. Our ability to recall where we've lived, the jobs we've had, and our personal behaviors all go into the evidence that adds up to having "told" and what science can claim. What diseases are reported to form the evidence varies by nation. In the US, Congress passed a policy to require the Public Health Service to collect morbidity reports on certain diseases in the late 1800s. At the time, this included smallpox, yellow fever, cholera, and the plague. A review of the Morbidity and Mortality Weekly Report published by the US CDC provides insights about current priorities.[135] Doctors and health care facilities have the responsibility to report these data. States may have additional priorities for which they collect data as well. This is true throughout the developed world. For example, to monitor the incidence of children's blood lead levels requires the collection of data in that regard. Data about cancer incidence helps guide the allocation of resources associated with cancer but requires reporting information about cancer patients. When disease registries don't exist for certain conditions or have great gaps in them, this feeds back into the seeming absence of a relationship between an exposure and our health. The truth is an absence of science to link to a claim.

Medical *research* depends upon our biological data. The goals of genetic research, for example, are met through both *recruitment* of participants to provide DNA, serum, and plasma samples, *and* through the use of a national repository of biospecimens. With the former, we have a choice. With the latter, not so much. For example, cancer tumors linked to clinical data may be used for research on clinical outcomes. Someone's age, weight, and biological sex, for example, may be known about a tumor that is included in research to learn about relationships between these variables and cancer. Many other possible relationships literally depend upon whether we have disclosed information about ourselves. If we withhold information, it contributes to greater reliance on single determinants within the scientist's purview, such as genes. Some exposures may be evident based on a specimen, such as the effects of smoking on lungs, but other exposures that have not been established need our *stories* to advance the scientific hypotheses. For example, if as a child you lived near an industry that was discovered to pollute the city's water source that you were raised on, your biological specimens may have a unique characteristic which will give scientists a novel way of thinking about causes of cancer or mutations.

Why don't we tell all we know about our health when it might serve the good of the many? We're often uncertain about how disclosing personal information may impact our employment, health insurance, personal and social relationships, and our own self concept.[136] So, we may avoid telling. Participating in public health activities and choosing to tell may be more likely when we know if and how our confidentiality will be protected. A lot of entities collect, store, and use our health information: doctors, hospitals, other health care organizations; insurers and employers; educational institutions; health departments; environmental departments; welfare and family services; social security; government disability. A patchwork of policies exists relating to whom doctors can legally tell information about our health: other doctors; epidemiologists or researchers. A patchwork of policies exists around computerized health information, as well, and the priorities associated with safeguarding our health information once it reaches health insurers. What we don't want to find after the fact is that someone got hold of our information and used it to limit our freedoms, which is a second issue related to treating health as a public good.

When Our Freedoms Are Limited

Be aware of what you give up to support the public's health and whether it benefits you.

Have you ever considered what you do and what you can't do because it's in the interest of public health? We've all given up some of our freedom to support health as a public good. Many of the things we do or don't do vary widely and often are hardly even noticeable. We are asked to wash our hands after using the restroom, especially if we're an employee. In fact, a reminder appears in nearly every fast food restaurant's bathroom, though I don't recall, however, seeing them in finer dining establishments' restrooms. We're asked to shower before we go into the public swimming pool. And we're sometimes asked to have our blood or other body fluids tested to promote health and prevent disease: testing of the breath, blood, or urine to evaluate the concentration of alcohol in the blood; drug testing if we want to be employed by any number of organizations; even after employment, random drug testing (air traffic controllers and other personnel working for the FAA in the US face this). An increasing number of public spaces limit or ban smoking. Often, public parks post signs that say, "No alcoholic beverages in the park." We can't carry guns to school or work. Speed limits, traffic signs, crosswalks, sidewalks, street lights – we invest a tremendous amount of our resources in infrastructure aimed at keeping us alive and healthy.

It's an unfortunate reality that we sometimes react with anger and the feeling that someone's taking away our right to control our own actions when our behaviors are restricted, even when the restriction is aimed at benefiting our own or others' health. This response doesn't take a vacation in the interest of pubic health. Indeed, if overused, we begin to feel that the whole idea of protecting the public's health by limiting our freedoms is a ruse or a ploy (e.g. seatbelts and motorcycle safety helmets). As with the behaviors prescribed to us as individuals to manage our health, some practices linked to behavior and public health are ones that we can too easily forget. So, while seatbelt use has largely been mandated, the excuse for failing to use them, that "I forgot, I'll put it on right now. Please don't give me a ticket," contributes to engineering solutions, such as passive seatbelt systems. It's an odd dynamic that we humans have created in this world of health as a public good. The debates illustrate the tension between communicating about the public good versus personal autonomy, and another path to stigmatizing individuals based on their health status or behavior. It's not enough that a smoker has to bear the identity of being neglectful of his own health, but in this context of health as a public good, the smoker is also "inconsiderate" as well if he puts the health of others at risk by exposing them to smoke.

In addition to limits on our behaviors, there are also actions we must comply with based on health as a public good. Sometimes, these policies are adopted by organizations. One of the most universal practices required of us to protect health are immunizations, often prescribed by laws. "School laws" name vaccinations such as diphtheria, pertussis (whooping cough), measles, mumps, polio, rubella as requirements for students to be in public schools. Many universities have requirements relating to college students and immunization as well. These policies are adopted in the wake of much discussion and debate once a disease has been named as serious and preventable by vaccine. From 1985 through 1992, data were collected by the Measles Surveillance System of the CDC and combined with annual state immunization program reports for youth aged 5 to 19 years. Exemptors were found to be 35 times more likely to contract measles than were vaccinated persons. In the US, exemptions are granted for religious and philosophical reasons, and have been found to cluster in certain geographic regions.[137]

While our personal behaviors may be both limited and prescribed in the name of public health, society also grants the authority to our peacekeepers to act for the public's good in order to preserve life and well-being. In the US, the number of lives lost to epidemics during the era when the Constitution was drafted contributed to granting states the power to regulate threats to public health in the form of "police power" authority. The early law enforcement departments included some responsibility for public health functions. Modern law enforcement agencies generally find the "police power" function inconsistent with day-to-day responsibilities. Police power grants public health officials the right to search and seize without probable cause, warrants, or prior court hearings. It also grants courts the right to defer to public health officials' discretion. This may include the use of quarantine, the isolation of persons with disease that can be easily spread.[138] Before vaccines, the first line of defense against disease was quarantine. Stockpiling supplies such as medicine and medical equipment may also be required in the name of health for the public good. So long as, for example, stockpiling flu vaccines doesn't prevent us from getting our flu shot due to too few available shots, we're likely to be supportive of having medications and supplies in secret locations which can move as needed within hours to support an emergency. The evident tensions between individual rights guaranteed in the Bill of Rights and police powers quickly become apparent, however, especially in an era of bioterrorism and broader terrorist threats to a nation. And the question becomes, "Is serving the public good benefiting my health here and now?"

Our freedom of expression may also be limited to support the public's health. Advertising for some products judged to be harmful is restricted as to where, when, and even how it appears. There has been international legal wrangling over expressive freedom and tobacco advertising. In the US, we don't see ads for condoms or tobacco on TV. The US alcohol industry limits itself by not showing ads for "hard liquor." While US advertisers limit *direct* advertising, the World Health Organization finds that advertisers spend three times as much on *indirect* promotional activities, such as contests, product tie-ins, and sponsorships, as they do on direct ads. Freedom of expression, thus, finds other avenues, ones that we may be less aware are there to influence us. Industries who have had limits placed on their efforts to sell products that harm our health also cultivate "front groups" to gain our support in getting government to remove such limits. In the US, for example, the tobacco industry financially supports the "Get government off our back" group – a coalition created by R. J. Reynolds in 1994 to fight federal regulation of tobacco.[139]

In the name of the public good, we may also be required to receive involuntary treatment. This isn't limited to psychiatric settings. End-of-life decision-making is prescribed as a means to promote the interest of the public. It's often religion that society uses to justify placing some limits on our personal autonomy in decisions about health. Officials who have the responsibility to define these limits face challenges about how to explain it when it violates our right to decide matters of life and death. If we don't make our wishes explicit, efforts to resuscitate us when that may not be our choice are likely. In society, religion as a process and spirituality as a way of looking at the world affect and are affected by government and governing. Both religion and government place limits on our freedoms relating to health as a public good. If we recognize this reality, we can act to preserve our wishes in many cases. We can also recognize that they contribute to how societies often define health as a public good to promote our safety.

When Safety Clashes with (E)Quality

Read product labels even when you think you know what they say. Participate in community efforts to set health standards.

Do you look for the posting of a restaurant's food safety inspection when you eat out? Do you think about the community swimming pool as a site for germs to be hiding? Do you wonder if your job site, apartment building, or the football stadium has had a fire inspection lately? Probably not, because we take for granted all the ways that the public's health in most developed countries is being looked after. All the ways that we are *safe*. When society organizes to promote the good of us all by working toward our health and well-being, safety emerges as a persistent theme. As with the experience of my granddaughter's preschool, we may think that it's all gone a little overboard, but then we may not be the ones with a child who has peanut allergies. To promote the public's safety, tremendous levels of resources and effort are directed at training, licensing, and insuring our safety across public domains. We only sometimes hear about a restaurant closing due to failure of a health inspection. Once in awhile, a public place like a water park has to shut down due to some health threat, such as E. coli bacteria in the kiddy pool. When I enter the largest football stadiums in the nation, I feel confident that the fire safety codes have been followed. But I recognize the challenges associated with making choices about training and licensing. There are tremendous redundancies in a system that is organized in the US at the state and local levels, and in other nations by regions or territories.

Do we really need every state to spend its time on developing an elaborate code of standards for licensed child care centers? Couldn't there be a set of guidelines to set out the general approach to such matters as fire safety, child abuse reporting, and the staff to child ratio? If a center wanted to do better than what is required, great. But that isn't how it works, of course. We rather enjoy the process of coming together and organizing around our perceived unique commonalities as well as differences. Or so it appears based on the endless products linked to standard-setting that bear similar titles but come from different locales. As long as we're willing to pay the cost, we can continue to emphasize our differences in this fashion. But at some point in considering the public good from an economic vantage, we citizens of the world may have to decide that less redundancy would be good. Which first requires that we recognize that it exists and why.

One important consideration across so many nearly invisible sites linked to health as a public good is training. This applies to child care centers. But it also applies to a long list of services we again take for granted. Safety is such a pervasive goal linked to health as a public good, we take it for granted – food, drugs, transport of hazardous wastes on public roads. The classic case of the meat we eat forced states to adopt their own laws in the US. This led to manufacturing nightmares as individual companies had to meet the standards of each state. It was Upton Sinclair's novel, *The Jungle*,[140] published in 1906 and describing conditions in Chicago's packing plants, that brought the issue to a head. As the pubic learned about practices, meat sales dropped severely. Only then did President Roosevelt shepherd a meat inspection bill through the US Congress. Hardly a day goes by that we don't hear about a case of health threats linked to food or drugs. Sometimes, these relate to an instance where someone has become sick even after inspection of foods. When this happens, review of the practices linked to inspection may prevent a future occurrence. An examination of training for those involved in the inspection will be part of the process.

The safety of the blood supply is another priority linked to health as a public good. Blood is named a pharmaceutical item in the US, for example, which places it under the purview of the Food and Drug Administration (FDA). The licensing of tests to screen the blood supply is an activity that the FDA governs through the Investigational New Drug (IND) application process for testing.[141] Interest in developing a test depends upon scientific evidence that a disease is transfusion-transmissible *and* warrants *commercial* efforts to devise testing. Tests for hepatitis B and syphilis, for example, have been conducted on each unit of donated blood since before 1985. These diseases emerged in epidemiological data as ones likely to threaten a large enough proportion of us to warrant the *investment* required to develop testing. Tests for HIV-1 (human immunodeficiency virus) and HIV-2, hepatitis C virus, and HTLV-I and HTLV-II (human T-lymphotropic virus) are conducted on the donated blood supply, as well.

Public resources to promote the quality of any nation's blood supply are limited, competing with all the other aims linked to the public's health. As we enter the end of the first decade of the twenty-first century, the policy in the US for many parasitic infections, such as malaria, is to rely on the potential donor to protect the quality of the blood supply.[142] Individuals who have visited malarial areas in the past year or moved from such an area within the past three years are *asked* to defer donating. Babesiosis is a parasitic infection that may be transmitted by tick bites, most often in the northeastern US. Here, too, potential donors are *asked* about a history of this infection. Those with such a history are permanently excluded from blood donation by some organizations, including the Red Cross.[143] Potential donors who have had Lyme disease, which is related to the bite of certain species of the deer tick, will be asked to recall if they've had the disease, whether they had a *full* course of antibiotic treatment, and whether they've had any further symptoms. Those who answer "Yes" to the first question must also answer "Yes" to the second question and "No" to the third question in order to be potential eligible donors. Notably, in instances where we depend upon communication as the strategy to support the quality of donated blood, if the individual donor does not know, cannot remember, or fails to disclose these conditions, blood safety may be compromised.

Beyond food and drugs, we largely depend upon government to act on our behalf to promote the quality of air and water. These clearly comprise elements that add to health as a public good. Health harms associated with air became a focal concern in the US in the second half of the twentieth century, leading to the Clean Air Act passed in 1963. My husband and I, together with our infant son, moved from the Midwest to California in 1978. "Smog alerts" were the norm every afternoon. I hadn't bargained for that, but at least they were making the effort to communicate about the risk so I could keep myself and my son indoors. There's definitely inequality in the levels of air quality throughout the world linked to population density, as illustrated in Copenhagen,[144] Los Angeles, Houston, and Atlanta compared to rural areas of Pennsylvania in the US. And there's also the reality that the industry polluters reduce the property values of homes nearby, making the likelihood of exposure to poor air greater for lower-income families who live there. The US Environmental Protection Agency estimates that we can blame poor air quality for one million cases of decreased lung function and 350,000 cases of asthma in children in the US.[145]

Water, too, is just one of those things I grew up never having to think about in terms of its quality. Then, while living in the Atlanta area in a nice middle-income subdivision, I received a request from the city utilities to provide a water sample from my home. I don't remember the details of the how and when and where the sample was provided, but I still have the report that came back with the results because it was frightening. We had moved into the home when our children were 10 and 13 years of age and so I immediately linked their development to the test results, which revealed normal levels of copper but highly elevated levels of lead. The report had an asterisk next to the lab test result for lead. It states that the US Environmental Protection Agency has established an "action level" of 15.0 µg/l for lead – micrgograms per liter.[146] The results of our test were 56.00 µg/l – nearly four times higher than the "action level." The report goes on to say

> Lead and copper may be found in household plumbing fixtures. . . . Lead is found throughout the environment in the air, soil, water, and pottery, porcelain, and pewter. . . . Lead and copper enter drinking water primarily as a result of the corrosion or wearing away of materials containing these materials. Lead can pose a significant risk to your health if too much of it enters your body.

Of course, they had me at 56.00 µg/l. The report does go on to tell the reader how to limit exposure. The recommendations include flushing the cold water faucet until the water is as cold as it will get to remove stagnated water. Using cold water for both drinking and cooking. Not using hot water for making baby formula. Not cooking or consuming any water from the hot water faucet.

The next time I encountered issues linked to the safety of water to be consumed was when my daughter started college. In this case, she was in one of the older dormitories and they stated in information given to us that water should not be used for drinking without filtering. Off she, her dad, and I went to explore options and make a purchasing decision. Since that time, our family has pursued consistent and aggressive efforts to filter our drinking water in our homes and when traveling. We'd already adopted the habit when we lived in Arizona and made frequent trips into Mexico for visits to the beach. But it now extended beyond our visits to other countries to our trips within our own country. In the US, the Clean Water Act, which originally passed in 1948 and is revised almost annually, gives the Public Health Service authority to develop programs to reduce or eliminate pollution of interstate waters, as well as improve sanitary conditions of surface and underground waters. The Safe Drinking Water Act, passed in 1974, reveals the extended boundaries of the debate. Farmers know to put their wells on the high side of the property so that the runoff from agricultural activities doesn't pollute their drinking water. We as a global society are having a more difficult time.[147] How do we filter the water that carries the runoff from all the products, including antibiotics and other pharmaceuticals and nutri-ceuticals (discussed in the next chapter), streaming out of us as waste products and into our water sources?

Beyond the many efforts formed to support the public's safety as practices and policies communicated to us as part of the communities in which we live and work, enormous energies are put into efforts to advise us of potential health risks with "warnings."[148] These come in the form of print materials quite often, although they may be included with a product purchase as a broadcast medium of some type. In either case, the benefit to be gained depends upon us to apply the content to our behavior. Product warning labels aim to lessen our uncertainty as consumers about using things in a safe manner. Governments mandate the structure of these messages in many cases. In the US, both the FDA and the Occupational Safety and Health Agency (OSHA), guide these

Figure 5.2 A photograph taken by the author while visiting Sydney, Australia.

efforts. Product warnings have four categories of information. They include a signal word, hazard statement, hazard avoidance statement, and consequences statement.[149] Signal words include "danger," "warning," and "caution" which is intended to get our attention and motivate us to engage the message. The challenges linked to getting our attention and our time to devote to safety have increased the use of pictures as a substitute for words to remind us of the desired behavior, as illustrated in Figure 5.2. The more we use a product, the less we notice its warning label. There may be more effective ways to gain our participation in efforts to promote health for the public good than having government impose limits on our freedoms or "engineer" our safety with warnings and regulations.

What Nonprofits Have to Do with It

Join a nonprofit group whose work to improve health for the public's good excites you.

Do we have a role to play in promoting the public's health? When it comes to efforts to support the public's health, government can't do everything. And, we hasten to add, we don't want them to. The reality of working for the good of us all in promoting health is that it only works when we participate – "we" being all of us members of the public. We're living in a time when volunteerism is up worldwide as we try to make a difference. It has become slightly annoying and even trite to listen to the stories of rich celebrities making a difference when most of us have been doing all we can in that regard for all of our lives. It starts with taking a plate of food to the elderly neighbor across the street; helping to get our friend's child to soccer practice, so he can participate even though his parents' work schedule makes it a near miss; cleaning and cooking and caring for neighbors and family. But the needs linked to these efforts have become much bigger than you or I can tackle on our own. As a result, there are new nonprofit organizations forming every day to tackle these issues and needs.

To assess what nonprofits bring to the table only requires that we look at the acknowledgment page of practically any annual report linked to a public health initiative. In the US, there we will find representatives from such groups as the American Cancer Society, the American Lung Association, the American Heart Association, the American Diabetes Association – the nonprofit organization representing the particular condition strives to be present and counted in these public initiatives. Parallels exist in many other nations, as illustrated in the UK, for example, with cancer patient care and advocacy organizations including Macmillan Cancer Support and Marie Curie Cancer Care. Their role as advocate is one that allows them not only to be involved in service delivery, educating the public, and research but also to engage in lobbying. Positive effects at societal levels have been achieved by nonprofits in advocacy for issues as varied as environmental concerns[150] and the care partners of people with AIDS.[151]

Nonprofits often form the backbone in efforts to promote the public's health. In part this occurs because they have potential to shape the political agenda and to garner resources for an issue. As a group matures, its understanding of the sociopolitical environment affects its potential for action. It takes some time to figure out how the system works. It takes some time to decide when to work within the system and when efforts may have to extend outside the system. While nations often set some limits on the amount of money nonprofits can use for lobbying, these groups are vital in the role they have to educate elected officials. It's unrealistic and impossible to expect representatives to be expert regarding each and every issue on which they have to vote. The gaps in understanding are filled in various ways, and nonprofits are one.

Nonprofit groups can sometimes become competitive. Some diseases have more organizations representing them than others. Sometimes, this can lead to conflict, to the desire to claim ownership of some tasks, and even create rivalry between groups. This can be especially frustrating for volunteers who often are either survivors of a condition such as cancer, family members, or those managing life with a condition. A communication approach to resolve these conflicts focuses on identifying a formal liaison between groups, someone with membership in both groups, to participate in both and guide a long-term perspective. It can be a key role for a committed volunteer.

Almost everyone at every age can find at least one nonprofit to join and become actively involved with. Use the lessons learned about yourself from Chapter 3 to suggest what might most engage your time and energies. What excites you? What worries you? Get onboard with those who have the same passions. My husband and I belong to the Juniata Clean Water Partnership,[152] a nonprofit organization aimed at advocating for improved water quality. The group works to clean rivers and to advocate for keeping them clean, often spending time on the water as part of the effort to see what needs to be done and to get motivated to do it, as seen in Figure 5.3. Participating in nonprofit groups that work to protect the environment and to advocate for groups affected by serious health conditions is a gateway to understanding and working within public health systems.

Why Public Health Matters

The next time you're online, explore how public health is organized and delivered in your community and nation.

Figure 5.3 The author's husband kayaking as part of a river sojourn with Juniata Clean Water Partnership.

What does public health mean and why should you care? Oddly enough, most of us don't know the answer to that question. Most of us simply don't know what public health does, how one goes about getting a job in public health, or if any of it matters to any of us in our everyday lives. This is a significant gap in communicating about health and health care, especially since public health is arguably a universal system of health care, a foundation on which to build more endearing and enduring programs to support well-being. In 1993, I met the "face" of public health in the US, a woman who was to become a life-long friend. She was nearly a foot shorter than me but had served in a role that required her to stand tall as she went toe-to-toe with men elected to positions of power through the votes related to budgets for public health in the state of Georgia. And yet, she had to remain diplomatic because she served at the "pleasure," as they say, of these elected officials as the Manager of the state's Cancer Control Program. Over the next decade before she retired, we would make many trips together around the state and attend meetings with various constituencies. I came to understand why public health matters.

I learned on those trips that in the days when she first started working for public health in Georgia, she got her pilot's license so she could fly to rural areas to deliver services. I learned that her devotion was and is not uncommon in the professionals and practitioners drawn to public health. And I came to understand something about the meaning of public health. The mission of public health is to assure conditions to support the public's health. Yet, talk about public health and medicine, or health care reform has seldom intersected. Partly, this occurs because public health is focused on populations while medicine focuses on us as individuals, and so the goals seem unrelated. In reality, however, doctors – who are viewed as an important source for health education and promotion – have little time to do either.[153] Instead much of what we know comes from public health and risk communication. These messages, in turn, often aim to enhance our understanding so that we will seek medical care when appropriate. So they often guide us into the medical system as needed. They often include, "Tell your doctor," as a prescriptive component.

Public health activities, both nationally and internationally, set the agenda for health. In these efforts, it's been shown that how the media talk about health often parallels the public health agenda.[154] When public health talks about the environmental risks relating to geological radon, media tell us about these risks.[155] When they talk about the flu and remind us it is time to get a flu shot, we're more likely to do so. When they tell us to boil our drinking water, because the rains have caused the city water to be unsafe for the time being, we listen. Unlike the voice of parents or bosses, these voices are mostly accepted in our daily routines and only found to be objectionable when we find our freedoms to be overtly threatened.

Public health attempts to fill the gaps for access to basic levels of health care, especially for women, children, and low-income citizens. Public hospitals are a major health service provider, an indispensable resource, offer few barriers to care, and respond to government mandated policies. Public system hospitals and clinics around the world, however, are often located in declining and poor urban areas. Too often, with too few resources, they have poor management. They are saddled with pauper stigma as their identity. Again, our lack of understanding about what public health is and who performs public health functions contribute to this status.

Public health efforts also establish norms for ethics relating to health.[156] Communicating about health as a public good often has moralistic overtones. Engineering related to products to support our health may be appreciated when it leads to less forgetfulness or just plain less effort on our part to protect our health – automatic seatbelt systems, cabs over tractors to protect farmers who would otherwise be exposed to sun, pesticides and increased risk of harm from rollovers. Social engineering to tweak our genes or in other ways intervene to control population health is harder to recognize. So, while we don't think much about the boundaries drawn around public health versus medicine, communication about health dances in these two domains so fluidly that even the experts can become dizzy with efforts to define them.

Summing It Up . . .

Clean air. Clean water. Clean genes? The eugenics movement seems largely to be forgotten among most citizens. Like so much good that is part of treating health as a public good, the bad parts of the process also get left behind in our imaginations. But the success of efforts to treat health as a public good depends upon our acceptance of a role. So we need to decide exactly what role we want to play in the process. The completeness of disease reports requires us to lend our literal blood, guts, and tears for examination, to be honest about what we know and to try to find out what we don't know. In the process, new identities may form, new ideas about who's responsible for health may emerge, and resources may or may not be allocated based on how public health as a public good is understood.

Communicating about newborn screening isn't very different from the communication that takes place around other data collected to guide decisions about the public's health. Quite simply, we often have no idea if and how information about our health is being used. As illustrated with my granddaughter's newborn hearing test, an expanded approach to newborn screening deviates from traditional criteria for screening which required that the disease be one that caused severe health problems, that testing be affordable and effective, and that there was treatment available for the condition. Babies are now being screened for a variety of metabolic conditions that lead them to be identified as "not normal." For some of the conditions for which testing is done, there's no treatment. This makes labeling a likely outcome, and stigma or discrimination possible.

We all have a suspicion or a nagging and lingering concern that data about our health are somewhere and somehow being used by someone. But efforts to communicate about health as a public good seldom tell us how this all works, including how our individual tissue samples are used. The reportable conditions may vary depending upon the country in which we live, but there are many common ones to promote the ability for cross comparisons and hypotheses linked to the public's health. And so we might wonder in this scenario and others, "Who profits from my health?" – a fifth question that may be used to frame communicating about health and its outcomes.

6

Who Profits from My Health?

One of my sisters was visiting and we were spending a couple of chilly nights watching movies from my collection. We watched the movie, *Outbreak*. It illustrates a town in which efforts to contain a deadly virus are extreme. I laughed to break the tension at a couple of points. When I said, "This isn't how it would be or how we would respond. It's too exaggerated" my sister responded, "Really? Why not? I know the script takes some liberties, but it's not really science fiction. So isn't it supposed to help us understand how these viruses work and what our nation's response would be if something like this happened? They have fact checkers, for the scripts, don't they?" I suppose I had a surprised look on my face, as she added, "I don't have time to keep up with all this health stuff. I count on movies and TV to be accurate."

I won't ever forget that moment. My sister is a college-educated woman with a full-time career, a husband, and family, including me, whom she wants to spend her free time with. She doesn't want to spend that time trying to decode a lot of medical research or even news reports about medical research. She's told me before that she doesn't really watch the news. And she's not alone. So what does that mean? The entertainment industry and advertising become resources used to fill in the blanks many of us have between the science we learned in school, what our doctors and social networks may tell us, and our need to know. For those of us who do watch the news, it adds another resource. So the bottom line is . . . the *bottom line*, because in all that talk about health, a tremendous amount of it comes from a profit motive.

Pharma-, Cosme-, and Nutri-ceuticals

Read the fine print – even if you have to get out a magnifying glass
to do it. Assume that use of pharmaceutical, nutriceuticals, and
cosmeceuticals *do add up*.

Are you looking for a cure to what ails you and your family? Newborn
suffering with teething pain. Toddler suffering from a cold. Young child
who's taken a tumble while learning to ride his bike. Adolescent with
her acne outbreak. Teen who spent too much time in the sun. Partner
who lifted the wrong way. Parents whose joints ache. Yes, we have an
endless list of reasons to be looking for relief. And that motivates creative minds to keep developing innovative pharmaceutical solutions.
Pharmaceuticals are all those drugs selected as treatments, many of which
are prescribed. Hundreds of billions of dollars in pharmaceutical sales
occur annually across the world. Pfizer in the US, GlaxoSmithKline
in England, Sanofi-Aventis in France, Novartis, in Switzerland, and
AstraZeneca in England were the top five sellers for 2007.[157] The top
three uses? Cancer, cholesterol, and respiratory agents. Then there are
the over-the-counter medications, OTCs. OTC drugs used in medical
care include painkillers, allergy prevention and treatment products,
antacids, antihistamines, laxatives, antifungals, treatments for asthma
and cold sores, cough suppressants, and a host of other products for which
you probably have your favorite few. European companies have strong
drug sales in Europe, including Germany and France, and also Japan.
But they also make sales in the US as they acquire product lines, including the analgesic market, the largest OTC category in the US with sales
in the billions of dollars each year.

Once a pharmaceutical innovation is ready for distribution, ads
appear in thousands of medical journals to keep our doctors up to date,
online as pop-ups linked to whatever information we're searching for,
and in grocery store aisles peering out from product packages. In the
US, we're also bombarded with direct to consumer (DTC) medication
ads on TV. Even as I write these words, the ABC "World News Tonight"
program in the US is being sponsored by just one advertiser for the evening, so that they can bring us more news without interruption. The
sponsor is Lyrica, which boasts the first FDA approved drug therapy
for fibromyalgia. DTC ads reach citizens in the US through TV, radio,

billboards, magazines, and direct mailings but aren't available in much of the rest of the world. Why? Because the ads are viewed as "biased," emphasizing benefits to the neglect of possible harms. One survey of hundreds of general practitioners and pharmacists in New Zealand, the other country besides the US where DTC ads are common, found that the doctors believed the ads could contribute to participative decision-making but were too often an *unreliable* source of information.[158] These doctors' impressions seem to confirm that it isn't so much a matter of too many ads but rather the content of the ads. Sometimes, it's good. Too often it isn't. Content is also a limitation of many product websites, which are universally accessible to internet users. These, too, de-emphasize side effects. In fact, the most common side effect is presented in online infomercials only about 70 percent of the time, and the top three side effects – about half the time.[159]

While the US FDA requires information about both risks and benefits to be presented in DTC ads, how to do it isn't prescribed. As a result of exposure to DTC ads, many consumers are able to recall names of drugs and the conditions to which they're linked, and ask their doctors to prescribe them. This reality has been observed for advertised anti-depressants[160] and other prescription drugs.[161] Many doctors *and* patients in the US feel that DTC ads lack important content needed to make informed decisions.[162] Drug companies pooh-pooh such claims and discredit those who make them,[163] but one thing's certain. There's profit to be made from selling drugs linked to our health.

Pharmaceuticals are just part of the picture for profits to be made relating to our health and a small part at that. In July of 2007, the Chinese government put to death a former director of its food and drug agency. Zheng had been found guilty of taking bribes in exchange for letting sub-standard drugs go to market, including the approval of six untested drugs. As a developing country, China doesn't have decades of experience in supervising food and drugs. But they have huge demand from citizens in their own country and nations around the world – all clamoring for China to produce large volumes of products for export – cheap. Pharmaceuticals, cosmeceuticals, and neutriceuticals head the list.

Cosmeceuticals are cosmetics for which a "drug-like" benefit is claimed. These products, which are applied to our skin, include an ingredient such as an antioxidant, vitamin, or enzyme linked to a health benefit claim. A growing list of moisturizing and anti-aging creams is among such products. A close look at labeling or packaging will show that they mostly haven't been clinically tested or approved by an organization such as the FDA. So, even for products that contain ingredients linked to positive effects in research, the cosmeceutical version often hasn't been rigorously tested to see if a topical form is effective. And no rigorous test to assess the concentration needed of a possibly effective ingredient likely exists. Warning labels, as described in the last chapter, appear on many of these products but not all of them. A list of ingredients, or at least "active ingredients," can frequently be found on the product or its packaging, though you may require a magnifying glass to read it.

Neutriceuticals are food extracts for which a "drug-like" benefit is claimed. The product is often presented in a medicinal format, including capsules, tablets, or powders. Innovative delivery systems include calcium-fortified orange juice. It is the health claims for the nutrient, calcium, which bring the orange juice into the realm of a nutriceutical. Nutriceutical sales have also reached billions of dollars worldwide, with indicators showing the Asia Pacific area leading sales. This includes Japan, China, South Korea, and Taiwan – all large consumers of fish oils, ginseng, and calcium among others. Combined with the functional food domain, where foods in our diet have links to physiological benefits *beyond* their basic nutritional function of fulfilling our need to eat, it all becomes quite complex for us as consumers. For three years, Kellogg included National Cancer Institute prevention messages in ads for All-Bran cereal and on bran cereal boxes. They found that consumers remembered the ads and bought the products because of the ads, which had a positive effect as well for Kellogg's profits. The findings motivated others to join, including Washington apples who had the ad "The original health food . . . High in fiber," and Campbell's Pork & Beans which chimed in with "Make more of a good thing . . . Twice the dietary fiber."[164] Soon, consumers find the market's cluttered with such approaches, so, not knowing what to make of it all, we may begin to ignore these health claims.

Food labeling has been one attempt to decrease the clutter and increase consistency for consumers. Years of debate in developed countries have guided the evolution of standards. The World Health Organization (WHO) and the United Nations Food and Agriculture Organization (FAO) formed the Codex Alimentarius Commission in 1963 to work toward recommendations for universal practices. The mutual goals of protecting consumer health and promoting fair trade practices for food internationally guide their suggestions of standards for food labeling. Countries like the US, Canada, France, and the UK spend enormous energies and other resources to advance best practices as well. The end results are food labels that can help us sort it all out if we use and understand them. Unfortunately, only about half of us even try to use them when making purchasing decisions.[165] Why?

Taking from my pantry a can of John McCann's Steel Cut Irish Oatmeal, a product from Ireland. I searched for the ingredients and found: "100 percent wholegrain Irish oats." Then off to the side are the "Nutrition Facts" including the size of serving I must eat to get the number of calories (including calories from fat), and grams for fat, cholesterol (zero), sodium (also zero), carbohydrate, and protein listed. Cholesterol and sodium (salt) connections to health harms may motivate a company to tell us when they *aren't* present in a product. Additionally, the content reports "percent Daily Value" (DV) fulfilled by eating one serving size when compared to a 2,000 calorie diet. Beneath a heavy dark line, the product label also reports the amount of Vitamins A and C – both 0 percent – while calcium is 2 percent and iron is 6 percent. In short, wholegrain Irish oats contain these things. They haven't been *added*. As part of a daily diet, eating this food will provide not just sustenance but what I would call small amounts of calcium and iron. I don't think anyone will be arguing for the use of this product as a functional food to supply calcium. On the other hand, it does provide 4 grams of dietary fiber, 15 percent of the DV, and some might want to argue for its merit as a functional food source of fiber. And so it goes.

Taking another product out of my pantry to compare with one that has had nothing added to it, I turn to my box of Kashi – The Seven Whole Grain Company's Oat Flakes and Wild Blueberry Clusters. Here, the list of ingredients began with oat bran – meaning that the product has more of this ingredient than those that follow in the list. Next came a long list of 24 other ingredients. Because these have been included, the product supplies 25 percent of the recommended daily amount of Vitamin A, 50 percent Vitamin C, and 100 percent of Vitamins, E, B6, B12 and folic acid. It also includes 10 percent of recommend zinc and iron. The oat bran has been *fortified* with some vitamins as ingredients added that may now make it a functional food. It has the American Heart Association "heart check" label on it, indicating that the product meets criteria for saturated fat and cholesterol. It claims on the front that it can help: "reduce cholesterol," "support healthy arteries," and "promote healthy blood pressure." Did this contribute to my purchasing decision? Yes, as a matter of fact it did. Would it contribute to yours?

Some nations make exerted efforts to communicate to citizens about food labels. In Ireland, for example, a campaign explained the difference between "Use by" and "Best before" labels,[166] as frequent inquiries convinced the government that consumers were confused by the two phrases. The former sets a date after which consumption may cause illness. The latter sets a date after which consumption may be disappointing in terms of quality but doesn't pose health risk. We've all had bread or other baked goods that get a little stale after a certain date. They were best consumed before that time. The US has an elaborate food label standard list but makes little effort to guide consumers' knowledge in this area. The standards define the meaning, for example, of a product's use of "high," "rich in," or "excellent source of" – such products contain 20 percent or more of the DV per RACC (Reference Amounts Customarily Consumed). A "good source," "contains," and "provides" links to content that is 10–19 percent of the DV per RACC. No campaigns explain these meanings to consumers. Do we understand? I didn't until I looked it up.

We also don't hear about how all these "ceuticals" to treat our health add up, interact with each other, or cause other conditions besides the one we aim to relieve. Aspirin is one example, as Reye's syndrome has been linked to aspirin use. This has guided the recommendation that no one under the age of 19 even use aspirin. We should assume that use of pharmaceutical, nutraceuticals, and cosmeceuticals all *do add up*. And we should look at the different ways we are delivering drugs or things that interact with them to our bodies as potential paths to an overdose. Take the example of aspirin. One can overdose on taking aspirin. One can overdose on taking other OTCs that contain aspirin. One can also overdose on applying cream to your skin that includes aspirin. A high-school track star who died in the spring of 2007 in the US is just one example of a consumer using a product, in this case to relieve her aches and pain from training, in combination with other products, unknowingly causing harm and, in this case, death.[167] The active ingredient gets absorbed through the skin and into the blood. Creams may have a much higher concentration than the medication. This has been found to be extremely deadly if ingested, which has happened with children. An overdose is also possible when using two products for different reasons. If I take aspirin for my headache, it may not even cross my mind that rubbing a cream into my achy joints is delivering more of the same drug into my bloodstream. And this reality isn't included in advertisements for those products which pay for our news. Nor does the "news" talk about the importance of keeping track of all the ways we deliver drugs to our systems until something dire happens and it's "news."

The News, It Is an Industry

Recognize that time and space limit what broadcast or print news tell us about health. When using online sources, seek in-depth news about health, including links to other resources.

Where do you first hear about a promising new medical study? Or the results of a new drug on some disease? To reach doctors and public health professionals, as well as leaders in agencies such as the CDC and the March of Dimes, medical research appears in academic journals. These include such titles as the *Journal of the American Medical Association, The Lancet,* and the *New England Journal of Medicine.* To reach us, some of the research gets reported in the news. A lot of it actually. An increasing number of news groups have medical or health or science reporters. Shows such as "Good Morning, America" include some news about health. Turn on the evening news or go to one of the round-the-clock news channels or even to online news sources and you're likely to get reports about health as well. They tell us about autism, heart attack, stroke, high blood pressure, cancer, diabetes, and other diseases.

We learn about health issues, products, or services in the news, often before we hear about it from our doctor. And this is true for all developed countries. One study of nearly 2,000 news stories being aired in local US TV newscasts during a *single* week in 2000 found that 10 percent of the stories addressed health. The two most common topics were information about specific illnesses or about healthy living. The stories were mostly less than one minute in length and offered no contrasting point of view.[168] They tell us about the latest way to deal with these diseases and conditions based on the medical research. And sometimes they poke fun at the way that we interpret and use the news, as illustrated in Figure 6.1.

Figure 6.1   A cartoonist's rendition of our response to medical research. Cartoon by David Horsey from the *Seattle Post-Intelligencer*, originally published on Monday, January 28, 2002. Reproduced with permission.

Covering health stories is *not* a purely altruistic motive aligned with keeping us informed. It's what keeps the advertisers and the news organization in business. Medical research and therapies in the news, just like advertising, may prompt us to go to the doctor's office or get something for what ails us. Or, it may support our decision *not* to go to the doctor and to visit the nearest drug store or discount retailer to get an OTC remedy. Thus, while an ad may push us to get a product, the news may pull us based on our belief that we have "learned" something new to benefit our health. But how often does it work that way? Since broadcast news is on 24 hours a day and seven days a week, there's a lot of air time to fill. There's competition to be the first to break a story. In the rush, with less time, there are increases in inaccuracies and inconsistencies. And despite the air time to be filled, not all stories get reported.

Why do some stories make it to the news desk and into our living rooms while others don't? As a business, news programs know who watches and, thus, who's their target audience. They select stories that seem likely to have appeal to the greatest possible number of people in their target audience, so that they'll stay in business. Advertisers will keep advertising and paying the bills for their show. Those advertisers, of course, have many options as to what they will select to develop ads for, and they're guided in their choices by the number of people affected by a condition in deciding whether to spend advertising dollars linked to the news to reach some segment of consumers. So that means that products that are manufactured in mass and can be delivered in mass get advertising dollars aimed at consumers. This affects our access to information about more durable medical products, as considered in a later discussion in this chapter.

When doctors consider what's reported about health in the news, they judge it to be sensationalized, incomplete, inaccurate, unbalanced, or misleading – just like their views of advertisements linked to products and services for health. Analyses of these reports suggest that doctors' impressions are often right. An examination of reports on network evening news in the US between 1968 and 1996, for example, found an increasing trend toward sensationalism.[169] News values contribute to the way that the science of health is communicated.[170] The "recency" value – occurrence of an event on the day, in the week or month of the story – guides the selection of material. The value placed on "facts and figures" gives the news authority. But news outlets also appear to value "negativity," a reference to the reality that controversy frequently generates interest in a story – and interest keeps an audience. Add these characteristics up, however, and you have "sensationalism." Content inaccuracies are also common in news reporting about health, just as so many doctors believe. One study of 116 press reports about mammography and breast cancer, for example, found 42 errors.[171]

A second shortcoming in news reporting about health is a lack of details about such important insights as where the study was published. In the 116 press reports about mammography and breast cancer examined for content accuracy, 113 cited a scientific study. Only 60 such studies could be found, however, due to a lack of details about where the publication appeared. The addition of a phrase such as, "According to a study published in the *Journal of the American Medical Association* this week, Harvard medical scientists, Jane Smith and Joe Brown, found . . ." would enhance the ability of consumers and others to locate the research. Space limitations may contribute to the fact that few newspaper articles about medical research include details about either the method used or the participants in the research.[172] Science writers usually include quotations from experts in their stories, averaging about three such quotes per story.[173] This supports the value that news places on "attribution."

When we do judge what is reported about health in the news, we may not recognize its shortcomings. For example, after news reports talked about a "breast cancer gene," many women increased efforts to seek information about their breast cancer risk. Many if not most women don't have a family history to suggest that they will have a gene that increases susceptibility. Thinking that they might and going to be tested may impose undue emotional and financial burdens on themselves and their families. On the other hand, the small subset from families with a striking incidence may benefit greatly.[174] Knowing our family history predicts when the former is more likely than the latter and vice versa. If news reports clarified these relationships, we might act on the news in more informed ways.

When we think about the news coverage of health issues, services, and products, we're not thinking about the layers of sources involved. Is the health source online or in broadcast or print news? Is the source the news anchor or a doctor? Is the source a medical researcher or pharmaceutical company? They combine in our minds as one frame for "the news about health." To be better consumers of health news, we need to take stock of this "source layering" and identify all the sources that make up a presentation of medical science to consumers.[175] Our ability to parse the various layers may lead to better understanding. It can at least guide valid judgments about the content's credibility. This same critical lens applied to health content in movies and on TV would increase our awareness of the actual source of our knowledge about health.

The Entertainment Industry

Consider how you conform to what you believe to be "good" habits relating to health because you *learned* it from watching movies and TV.

How many movies have some content about health in them? How often do we recognize that our favorite TV drama and soap opera and situation comedy stars are dealing with health problems that affect our views about what we can do? In fact, our sense of whether we have control over our health is often a lesson we learn based on entertainment productions. Recall my sister's reaction to the movie *Outbreak*, described at the beginning of this chapter. In one study conducted to assess how the movie affected viewers, it was found to decrease belief in our ability to have control over health and increase belief in chance outcomes[176] – not ideal outcomes for communicating about health. In some of the research I've led, movies were found to emerge as the most frequent answer to the question, "What is the FIRST media message or image that comes to your mind when you read the phrase, 'genes and health.'"[177] Among 467 participants who responded, 107 responses were in the movie category. Of these, 14 had a general answer, such as "a science fiction" movie or a "cloning" movie. But 33 different movie titles were also named. These included *Gattaca, Jurassic Park, The 6th Day, The Blob, The Fly, Erin Brockovich*, and *Hollow Man*.

Beyond the movies, many of us use entertainment TV to keep up with health information. Most of us watch TV shows at least a few times a month. In the US, half of us watch two or more times a week. More than half of the regular viewers report they trust health information in the shows to be accurate. About one fourth say primetime entertainment TV shows are among their top three sources for health information. And about half report learning from daytime TV shows as well.[178] In our work regarding genetics and health, there were 82 participants who named TV sources. These included "ER," "X Files," "South Park," and "Life Goes On."

When it comes to TV, of course, not only the fictional content exposes us to influence but even with TiVo, traditional ads reach many of us through this medium. This is especially true for children who aren't as adept at dropping in and out of programming when ads appear. An analysis of 1,098 ads shown during after-school TV programming found that 36 percent were based on fast food restaurants, 17 percent were for candy, 14 percent were for cereals, and 2 percent for snacks.[179] Even more challenging to recognize, product placement ads help reduce the cost of production as products are deliberately placed into production – on TV and in the movies – in exchange for fees that add up to billions of dollars.[180] In the movie, *Superman II* released in 1980, Superman jumps through the side of a truck carrying cases of Marlboro cigarettes. In the movie, *Beverly Hills Cop*, released in 1984, Eddie Murphy has a scene in a warehouse filled with cases of Lucky Strike cigarettes. In the movie *Who Framed Roger Rabbit?*, released in 1988, Betty Boop has a scene where she's carrying a tray of Camel cigarettes.

Gwyneth Paltrow and Ethan Hawke feature Kool cigarettes in a scene where they're playing cards in the movie, *Great Expectations*, released in 1998. And Jim Carey features Marlboros in the movie, *Me, Myself, and Irene*, released in 2000. So over two decades, cigarettes have just been part of the scene in some of our favorite films. And, of course the products aren't limited to cigarettes. One of my favorites is, Aquafina bottled water in the 2004 movie, *National Treasure*. Nicholas Cage holds a bottle up to his forehead so he can peer through it to decipher text on the money in his hand. The bottle is placed just so we the viewers get a clear reading of the product label. I don't know about you, but I've never been in a *clothing* store where they had the counter next to the cashier filled with bottled water for sale. In fact, most such stores won't let you carry a beverage in, because they don't want to risk you spilling it on the clothing for sale there. One internet site that keeps track of what brands and products appear in these entertainment outlets is brandchannel.com.[181] The site is produced by Interbrand[182] who aims to help clients *be the best brand they can be*.

The effects of product placements in entertainment venues are far-reaching in part because we may have lower levels of awareness about these influences.[183] While direct advertising often uses the science of health to sell products, more indirect product placement methods require our effort to locate their intention. Is it an accident that the character's soda can is turned toward the audience so they can see the name of the product being consumed? Is it an accident that a cigarette package lies next to the hands of an actor playing a game of cards with friends – turned outward toward the audience so they can make out the brand name? Is it an accident that the bar at which the actors playing a romantic couple sit includes a certain kind of vodka or gin with the label displayed to the audience? In Jerry Seinfeld's situation comedy, his kitchen cabinets don't have any doors on them. Products line the shelves, their labels frequently clearly displayed.

Health content in entertainment includes inappropriate role modeling, as well as unhealthy products. In the US in the early 1990s, about one fourth of fictional programming during primetime had at least one use of tobacco in the episode, with 90 percent of the portrayals showing pro-tobacco use.[184] In New Zealand between 2002 and 2004, one in four TV programs was found to include positive images of tobacco use, the same percentage as found in the US analysis a decade earlier.[185] TV programming in the US reveals even more frequent use of alcohol, with consumption appearing in about half the programs at the end of the twentieth century.[186] Poor nutritional habits are also commonly portrayed, a partial explanation for findings that watching more TV correlates with elementary children's poor eating habits in the US.[187] In truth, the habits of the characters are so integral, the products they use so much just a part of who they are that we don't recognize how we're being influenced. And while poor habits are often portrayed, their effects are not. A review of more than one thousand major TV characters drawn from 1999–2000 primetime fictional programming in the US found just 14 percent of females and 24 percent of males to be overweight or obese, less than half the percentages of the general population in the US.[188]

Debate ranges widely about the effects of product placement ads and possible restrictions.[189] In these debates, the focus is on "dangerous" products and services, such as gambling, alcohol, and tobacco, to the neglect of content about health conditions, treatments, and therapies we learn from entertainment venues. We also get exposed as viewers to options about which we have no awareness until viewing them in these entertainment outlets. We learn about infertility treatments on prime-time dramas such as "The Practice," HIV prevention on soap operas such as "General Hospital," alcohol relapse on "ER," drug addiction and cancer survivorship on "Desperate Housewives." And our choices are affected, together with our knowledge and attitudes. One program in the US designed to leverage this reality is Hollywood, Health & Society[190] which provides entertainment industry professionals with accurate information for health storylines and recognizes some programs with awards for excellence in this area. TV, as a venue for entertainment education, or edu-tainment, has had some positive effects on health behaviors.[191] Entertainment portrayals also provide an opportunity to introduce viewers to options for health not linked to the "ceutical" industries. These options may not be choices for mass markets and go unnoticed without introductions via entertainment venues.

Band-Aids, Crutches, and More – Oh My!

Explore other products and services used to promote health besides the "ceuticals" but do so with a "profit-colored" lens.

How many products do you count on for your health besides the ones in your medicine cabinet? Over the years, I've come to rely on a few. Most recently, they had to do with putting my shoulder out again. It'd been happening with increased frequency. This time, we were on vacation. I couldn't bend over and pick up my three-year-old granddaughter. It simply hurt too much. I tried to keep it immobile. I tried to dull the pain with OTC meds. My mom suggested a pillow. She and one of my sisters had been sleeping with special pillows for years. My husband left our vacation spot and drove into town to hunt down a pillow. He came back with one and I gratefully tried it. I was getting really tired of not sleeping. It helped. But only a little. I still couldn't pick up my grand-child. Because my shoulder seemed best if I absolutely immobilized it, my husband went again into town, this time to hunt down a sling. I wore it the rest of our week-long vacation on the beach.

When we returned home, it wasn't getting any better. That was a first. In the past, it seemed to flare up and then be calmed by my careful efforts. I got to the point that I was in a meeting and literally had to turn my entire upper body in my chair to look towards someone calling my name. "What's wrong?" "Stiff neck." That afternoon I called the doctor and got in to see the nurse practitioner the next day. She was the gatekeeper in getting to see the doctor or other resources. She quickly ordered x-rays and gave me a prescription. She also recommended some physical therapy. I remember that even the way she offered it was different. She said something like, "If you want to learn how to deal with this for the long term, you probably need some physical therapy." Of course I wanted to deal with it for the long term. Did she think I liked being in pain? Then, yikes, I thought. Time out of my day. One more reason we like the medication route. Doesn't take much time to swallow a pill. Lucky for me I didn't really know how much time it was going to take and for how many weeks and that then I would have learned some new habits that I have to keep for life or expect problems again.

I called the physical therapist and learned that the first appointment each day was at 8 a.m. "I'd like that one," I said. Two days later, I was at the physical therapist's office. There was all kinds of "stuff" that happened that day. Ultrasonography. Careful stretching. Deep muscle heat treatment in a dark room. An hour and a half later, I was taped up in ways that allowed me to move more freely than I had in weeks. I walked out with a couple of assignments to carry out before our next meeting. One was to buy a kitchen timer and to get up and move every 30 min-utes. Another was to assess my work station. How I was sitting. What support I had for my wrists and arms up to my elbows. It didn't take long to find some ways I could help myself with changes to some of my habits.

The x-rays came back. I had bone spurs in the neck area. I was going to physical therapy two or three mornings a week. I was adding more exercises to my new routine. I was able to have the tape permanently removed and not just replaced. And I was using a device that I lay in for ten minutes at a time and pumped up in a way that stretched my neck to relieve some of the pressure on the bone spurs. As the weeks passed, I observed others coming for their appointments and found it interesting that so many of us had some of the same basic things to learn or relearn about how we stood, sat, and worked. I wondered why no one ever talked about these things in stories about healthy lifestyles. I thought about how the factory workers on the lines had frequent breaks in their workday and that workers in the information age hadn't continued the practice for various reasons. Just as the workers on the line needed to stretch and move around, we computer workers need to break and stretch and move. Eventually the physical therapist suggested that the device I was using for my neck would be likely to be approved by my insurance if I was willing to continue my routine and include it at home. "Sure," I said. My primary care doctor received the physical therapist's report and recommendation and approved the product's purchase, which then went to the insurer. It was approved and is now part of my healthy lifestyle.

Why are there no news reports about these sorts of aids for health? It's partly a numbers game. As described in relation to *who* advertises *what* in support of news programming, mass markets increase the likelihood that a product will be advertised. And the mass markets have mostly been defined in terms of the "ceutical" world. But it's also partly a kind of turf war, or a clash over identities. Doctors have been trained to understand how our bodies interact with all kinds of drugs and to know when "to cut." That's their business, if you will. So while they may object to being called "pill-pushers," they at least identify with it based on their education and professional identity. This is not the case when it comes to many of the more durable goods linked to health. These are more likely to be part of the identities linked to being in the applied health professions. But medical doctors still frequently have the authority to act as gatekeepers to our access or even awareness of all kinds of products for health care, including the device I use to keep my neck as healthy as I can.

These products are not making their way into entertainment or ads at the same rate as pharmaceuticals have. Nonetheless, they're appearing. The Johnson & Johnson company featured a 60-second TV ad on Thanksgiving Day in the US in 2007 for a Cypher stent, a device that is permanently implanted in a blocked artery to open it up for blood flow. Doctors have criticized the ad for its failure to warn consumers about dangers.[192] Surgeons may have more than one option in treating a patient. Once a course of action has been decided, should the patient debate the merits of the choices from surgical gloves to surgical instruments to devices with the doctor?

Sometimes, our knowledge about what advertising, news, and entertainment industries "sell" relating to health should extend to our awareness of *what's missing*. Low vision is another industry linked to millions of us worldwide who just can't see that well. I can't remember a single news report about living with low vision, which could be sponsored by the products designed to assist with it. I certainly have no movie images of someone using magnifying devices to read or glasses with viewing scopes built in. Low mobility occasionally appears in ads for products to be added in our homes if we can no longer climb stairs to a second story, or for scooter chairs if we have problems getting around outside the home. But there is a wide range of products for arthritis, for back problems similar to my neck problems, and for home care. Industries form around each. There are profits linked to each and lifestyles as well. But we mostly lack advertising, news, or entertainment stories or statistics to guide our awareness and we don't have any role models to observe, prompting us to ask about these alternatives. Not thinking and not knowing about ways to be healthy beyond drugs, cosmetics, and nutrition contribute to our health illiteracy, the inability to comprehend and act on information related to health decisions. So somebody's making a profit from contributing to our poor health and guiding our decisions related to good health simply because we don't know any better.

Who Benefits from our Health Illiteracy?

Teach your children well.

Health illiteracy is our inability to understand and use basic health information. It causes us to misuse medication because we don't know what instructions mean when they say things like, "Take 2 tablets 3 times daily." It causes us unintentionally not to follow our doctors' advice. As suggested throughout this book, there are a number of dimensions linked to our abilities in this realm. Perhaps they emerge most starkly when we look at communicating about health from a profit angle. But they connect back to how we use both numbers and stories to make sense of our health status and what to do about it. And the idea that someone's making a profit from our health illiteracy, that gets our attention. We don't benefit. Society doesn't benefit. And in truth, taking the long view, none of the "ceutical" innovators or makers of durable medical goods benefit.

There are a couple of dimensions to profit and our health illiteracy. If we buy products because we've made an uninformed choice, the profit nonetheless goes into the pockets of those in the business. However, drug companies certainly don't want us to use medications incorrectly because it only feeds into the potential harms linked to a drug therapy. In the long run, that doesn't benefit their bottom line. The same holds true for all business and industries linked to marketing products to us and our doctors to support health. So, why aren't they doing more to support the basic skills to decrease actual and potential harms. In truth, I'm not sure that many companies recognize that the *basic* reading, writing, and arithmetic once touted as primary content in public school have been lost in the translation to the twenty-first century.

Both familiarity and practice contribute to skills. At the reading level, I have no awareness of any school in the world where students use product or warning labels to practice reading skills. Why not? They will certainly face enough of them in their lifetimes. And when it comes to writing, the more we become familiar with persuasive devices, the ways to use language, the implicit versus explicit conclusions that can be imbedded in communication, the less we are influenced by advertising appeals. And the math skills, sometimes referred to as numeracy abilities, needed to cope with everyday living, not just in the health domain but across all areas of our lives, have probably more than quadrupled over the years.

We don't talk about our illiteracy in these ways, but we can't put the brakes on others making profit from our *lack* of skills if we don't start. We don't compare what our parents and grandparents needed to know and do with numbers, for example, to what we need to be able to do. Instead, what we hear in news reports, if we hear anything at all, is that our math skills have declined. For three decades, comparisons between

US and Japanese students' performance in math have shown Japanese children to perform better.[193] These differences are the result of the emphasis given to math skills in the two nations. Japanese students consider learning to be a filial duty,[194] with interdependent family relationships ranking high in motivations linked to actions. The US mantra associating education with achievement emphasizes the individual. This doesn't mean a lack of math skills, as savvy entrepreneurs in business and industry don't depend on others to translate the bottom line. Still, in many ways, the US has done little to link math ability and skills to goals and motivations.

The same goes for our reading and comprehension skills, and it carries over to health domains. For example, one survey of 2,659 patients in two large urban hospitals conducted at the end of the twentieth century found 60 percent couldn't understand a standard informed consent document.[195] Have you looked at an informed consent document? Beyond the fact that you may need a magnifying glass to see the text, the language used seems to be for the lawyers, not us. Many of us can read, but we lack other skills needed to sort through the meaning.

Informed consent documents, like the ones parents sign before their children get shots, usually contain technical terms *and* quantitative expressions. In the US, a report funded by the National Science Foundation (NSF), as part of a Center for Learning and Teaching found that, as of April 2007, just nine states required Geometry to attain a high school diploma, while 19 states required Algebra I, and two states required Algebra II.[196] In the twenty-first century, citizenship in the US – not just health decisions – should demand competence in geometry, algebra, and statistics. Geometry enhances our *logical* reasoning and *deductive thinking* skills, both critical in our efforts to understand risk. It also furthers our ability to discover patterns and relationships. As I went through elementary school in the 1960s, algebra was still referred to as "the new math," but that is far from reality at this date. So we need to stop talking about our declining math skills across citizens of the world and start talking about an incline, needs for *higher* levels of skills than ever before.

The numbers of science writers has grown as the science to report to us has grown. They consult with advertising firms. They get jobs working with news shows. And they acknowledge time and again that to improve the public understanding of medical research news, they have to clarify statistics and scientific terms, qualify stories about experiments, and report about the barriers to developing therapies for our health. Our health illiteracy causes science writers to censor themselves in their writing. They avoid stories that don't have proven human applications, such as rat research. They believe these stories raise false hopes and promises.[197] This form of self censorship may seem admirable to some. But another way to approach the problem is to take the time and space to develop brief inserts to include with such reports. Space limitations in news stories require that we ask for this content. It must be elevated to content of importance, content we seek. Such a strategy might improve health literacy rather than limit our opportunities for health and health care advocacy in promising areas.

Summing It Up . . .

Is it a conspiracy between health care, drug companies, and journalists to make a profit and stay in business by exploiting our health? It's certainly become "normal" for us to look for drugs, creams, lotions, and potions to relieve our every unwanted ache or pain. And, while many nations around the world limit DTC ads, they don't limit the health content that appears in the news. News stories give publicity to health issues, products, and services. Publicity is usually a strategic endeavor paid for by those seeking a profit. In such cases, advertising content and presentation are directly controlled by the sponsoring organization. The difference between advertising those "ceuticals" and news stories about them, however, boils down to who controls the content. News organization and reporter? Or sponsoring organization? It often is hard to tell the difference between the two.

Product placements in entertainment venues also expose us as viewers to health information, services, and products – options which we may have no awareness of until viewing them in these entertainment outlets. In reality, the questions of who's to blame for the powerful effects placements may have and who's responsible for understanding the profit motives in entertainment come to a focus on media literacy. We mostly frame medication as something to benefit our health, so we may more mindlessly respond to communication about it. We're not on our mental guard when health services and products come into scenes and settings for entertainment the same way we may have learned to be when alcohol use is being portrayed. To get out of that mindset will take effort. As with any habit, we have to apply intention and *want* to judge how we are being persuaded to choose and use "ceuticals," or any other possible profit-making device linked to our health.

We lose sight of what are *normal* life transitions in all the talk about health linked to giving us the news, entertaining us, and selling us the goods. We may even become addicted to the feeling that a medication can produce and go looking for it to create excitement, as discussed in Chapter 3. And we're none too happy if our doctor doesn't recommend it or our family won't support us in getting it, as suggested in Chapter 4. It may even be a public health message like those described in Chapter 5 that sends us to the doctor looking for relief, leading us to judge our doctor in a bad light if she doesn't recommend a particular treatment to us. Yet, what if we cause ourselves unintended harm by over-consuming, mindlessly using products that add up or interact with each other? Some cases, such as preparing to have a colonoscopy, require not taking aspirin for some days before and after a procedure. Some doctors or labs provide patients with a list of common medications with aspirin, because there are so many. We can't count on others to do this for us, however. Reading labels for ourselves is best. Only we know what all the products are that we use. In the end, it's up to us to take a look, a very close look, at what's in those health foods and cosmetics, together with the medicines we use. One thing's certain, all of these domains depend on what research has been funded, who has been funding it, and our own willingness to be actively involved. It requires an answer to the question, "What's politics got to do with it?"

7

What's Politics Got To Do with It?

I've given my informed consent to participate in medical research twice. Once for a surgical procedure and once for a drug therapy. My first participation was in a study of laparoscopic surgery for endometriosis, the condition my daughter-in-law had that was described in Chapter 4. I remember when I was asked to participate in the research, I had several thoughts. First, "How can I say 'no' when I ask people to participate in research all the time?" Then, "So this is what it's like to be asked. I have a million questions. And so little time." Because despite the fact that the research nurse asked me if I had any questions, she wasn't making eye contact with me, a sure sign she was hoping I'd just sign the form she was holding out to me.

The verbal description of the research given to me went something like, "We would like your permission to record your surgery for research purposes." The written form was more technical and needed a medical dictionary to understand. The most pressing question I had was, "Will anyone be able to identify *me* based on the images photographed for the research?" After all, it seemed to me that something was going to appear on that camera besides just my internal organs. I might not have been so worried if it hadn't seemed like it would be a picture of my "private" parts. I bet a lot of us would have the same reaction in the same situation. But perhaps not everyone would ask. Instead many of us would just decline to participate. Of course, those of us who are asked to participate in medical research might be considered among the lucky few. Because there's a lot of *politics* involved along the way between an idea about a new drug or treatment, and testing it in clinical settings.

Politics is a process, though we don't often think of it that way. It's how people make decisions about *who* gets *what*. We most commonly think about this in terms of governments, but we all know politics also affects these decisions in corporations, in academia, in religious settings, and even in families. Family and office politics differ from government politics, but both determine what topics get formally discussed, debated, and included in the public record, whether it's a family's "mental notes" about who does what chores and for what reward, the notes from a department meeting, or the Congressional Record.

When it comes to communicating about health, the public record is represented by published research. In the more than 150,000 articles about medical research published each month in more than 20,000 biomedical journals,[198] there's "politics" associated with the review process. Each journal has a set of reviewers identified as the editorial board and an editor who selected those reviewers. To avoid politics linked to stifling the voices of researchers, manuscripts may receive a "blind" review. Author identity is removed from the manuscript and authors aren't told the identity of their reviewers. The process is intended to avoid the influence that might be linked to knowing that a paper being reviewed was written by someone with an established reputation *or* someone with no reputation at all.

Submission of an article reporting the results of medical research is the *last* hurdle on the way to becoming part of the public record. Prior to that, there's an almost endless list of ways for research questions to be diverted and voices to be stifled. The priorities of both political and religious agendas set the stage for many funding decisions, both in the delivery of health services to citizens and the medical research to be done. That's a big prize, so, not surprisingly lots of voices try to be heard. These include all the businesses and organizations that depend on medical research dollars, the researchers, and us, as patients, advocating for choices we support. Looking downstream at the health and medical disparities that can be traced back upstream to decisions about what research to fund, the effects are, quite simply, the difference between life and death.

Medical Research and Disparities

Pay it forward. Participate in clinical trials.

Why do some groups have more options to treat their health conditions than others? How do we make sure that people like us aren't the ones left out? These are the questions most directly linked to the outcomes of medical research for our health and well-being. When I was asked to participate in the study for endometriosis treatment, I asked the research nurse recruiting me about my physical privacy. I was assured that nothing externally would be captured in the images to be used for the research. I was told I could even see the recording made of my surgery if I wanted to, and I later viewed it. That gave me a better sense of what had been done to me in my medical procedure and also what the researchers were studying. They were looking at the ability of the doctor to move around my internal organs and remove the overgrown uterine lining when using a small surgical incision in my abdomen and a scope rather than a larger abdominal incision.

Medical research depends on our participation. If we don't participate, what will be offered to us for treatment may be based on research that didn't include anyone like us. Or, we may not be offered some options because we, or someone like us, didn't participate. So, not participating creates some disparities in the body of medical evidence on which to base health care. Yet, far fewer of us participate than are eligible to participate.[199] Why don't more of us participate? None of us wants to be the "guinea pig" or "lab rat." We've joined in our minds the notion of research with images of labs and small animals being treated – well – inhumanely. And we don't want to be that. There's a long phase which usually lasts for years when new therapies *are* tried on animals in labs. Then there's a long process linked to regulatory review to justify taking a therapy out of the animal lab and into human studies. In fact, a relatively small percentage, often less than 1 percent, of the ideas tried in medical research labs make it out of that lab and onto our stage. When they do, the human studies are called clinical trials. They've come out of the lab and into the clinic. They're tried out on humans and the studies are "on trial" – to prove that they have benefit far greater than possible harm.

Medical therapies that move out of the lab setting into human trials must be approved by regulatory agencies, such as the FDA in the US, and are monitored by Institutional Review Boards (IRB) who watch closely to assure that human participants are being protected.[200] *Phase I* studies are conducted with a small number of *healthy* volunteers when the trial is for a new drug and a small number of affected persons when the trial is for a medical device or surgical procedure. IRBs focus very close scrutiny on our welfare when reviewing protocols for these studies and demand that investigators disclose any potential known harm related to a study. They also require immediate reports of harms that occur which may not have been foreseen. The latter is, in fact, the goal of Phase I research. Does something unexpected happen when humans use a new approach, such as a new drug, that didn't happen when the animal research took place? On occasion, patients rather than healthy volunteers may participate in Phase I trials. This usually happens when the patients have no other treatment options and have end-stage disease. I've known several pancreatic cancer patients who took part in such trials. Through their participation, they felt they were doing something for the rest of us even if they knew that benefit for themselves was a very long shot.

If a new therapy doesn't reveal any unexpected harmful effects on humans, a *Phase II* study may be undertaken. To do so, however, requires a new review by regulatory agencies and IRB. It's a new study and arguments to conduct the research must be supported by evidence from the Phase I studies. In Phase II studies, a relatively small group of patients – but more than the number usually involved in Phase I studies – are recruited to participate. Participants have the medical condition that the therapy is expected to benefit. Once they're recruited into the study, they'll be randomly assigned to receive the new therapy or not. This is a place where we get put-off when it comes to participating – being told that we will be "randomized to treatment." In our own research with efforts to understand how to recruit more cancer patients into clinical trials, we learned that how randomization is explained to patients often keeps them from participating.[201] A common way to explain it is to say that the decision about what group a participant will be in is made by a process that is "like the toss of a coin. Heads gets one therapy and tails gets another." For some, this sounds like gambling, and most people don't want to gamble with their lives, so they don't participate.

The goal of a Phase II study focuses on seeing if the new drug or procedure or device has the expected benefit, so part of the process is to compare it with a control group. Needless to say, if we agree to participate in medical research, we would like to think that there will be some benefit for us to do so. It seems hard to imagine what that benefit might be if we're going to be given a "sugar pill" – a placebo which looks like the new drug being tested but has no known biological effects. Even with surgical procedures, a control group may have a surgery where nothing besides the incision is actually done. In one Phase II controlled trial involving 165 patients, for example, arthroscopic surgery for arthritis of the knee was studied by comparing patients who received only a skin incision to those who had dead tissue removed or those who had blood and other fluids flushed out of the area.[202] Results showed no differences in function or pain levels over the following two-year period between the three groups. So taking the long view, the benefit is that non-therapeutic surgeries won't be performed. To get to that point, however, some patients had a surgical incision performed, and then nothing was done beyond that. If a surgical procedure being studied turns out to be beneficial and I received only a placebo or another approach that wasn't as effective, I could return in the future to receive a procedure – confident that it has *real* benefits.

If you're thinking, "I knew it. I'll never participate in medical research! Let somebody else go under the knife for the fun of it. Let somebody else take a sugar pill to prove the drug works." Three things for you to consider – in addition to remembering that science forms the boundaries for what your doctor talks about as options for your care. *First*, for most major conditions, such as a cancer diagnosis, there is a *standard of care* for treating patients. So, for many studies, the control group being compared to the new treatment receives the accepted standard of care – *not* a placebo. This is called an "active control." When you're recruited to medical research or trying to find a trial in which to participate, it's reasonable to ask whether the comparison group receives the accepted standard of care. If not, why not? *Second*, sometimes there are important reasons to include only a placebo for comparison *or* both an active control and a placebo condition. In these cases, researchers *exclude* those of us who would be put at risk by not receiving the standard of care right away. Think about this from their point of view. It doesn't do them any good to have a study in which patients are harmed by the research. So realize that there's a long list of inclusion and exclusion criteria to participate in medical research. Which means, of course, that the scientific method itself can contribute to some disparities in medical research. Individual lives are complex and health status usually includes more than a single condition. As we attempt to control for differences, we quickly find that it's impossible to rule out all the biologic transitions associated with being human: what we ate yesterday; when we last consumed alcohol; whether we're smokers. But medical researchers do carefully consider these and do their best to make judgments about participants who will benefit, not be harmed. *Third*, researchers expose participants for the *shortest* amount of time possible to test the new therapy. It's a data-driven enterprise. They're not looking for effects across time in this phase of study. They're looking to see if something new works.

When a drug or other therapy moves into a *Phase III* clinical trial, many more participants will be recruited to participate in a randomized, double-blind study. Once again, the research goes for regulatory and IRB review before advancing to this next stage. There must be convincing evidence that the benefit is likely and that any harms that may have been identified are far less than the possible gains. Once more, neither the patient nor the researcher will know whether the new drug or control – either active or placebo – is being given to the patient. Here, too, we as participants should ask whether the Phase III study is using an *active control* rather than or in addition to a placebo.

Phase IV research studies monitor the longer-term effects of a new therapy. This follows regulatory approval to take a new product to market. As suggested by the previous discussion of the phases leading to this point, getting to market is often a very long process.[203] Once it's there, you may hear about "after market" research. When a product is being used by us and, suddenly, there's lots of media attention given to it with reports about problems with the drug, surgical procedure, or medical device, it may be based on a Phase IV study, or it may be based on patient experiences and stories, as discussed in Chapter 2. This was the case for the drug Phen/Fen, for example, which was used in prescription diet pills and found to harm the heart,[204] so it was withdrawn from the market in 1997.[205]

In the medical device arena as well, there are worldwide efforts to regulate safety and effectiveness. Doing so requires controlled medical research. One difference between clinical trials for drugs and medical devices is that Phase I trials for the latter will generally require the use of patients intended to benefit from the device. The sample will be very small, as when one trial of an implantable middle ear device for hearing loss involved just five patients.[206] Positive results of the feasibility study contributed to further study. Japan has taken some leadership in the area of regulating medical devices through clinical trials. As the US and other nations have become consumers of Japan's growing medical device market, protocols with phases much like what's done with drug development have been approved. Why nations besides the US have taken the leading role in medical research relating to medical devices, while the US has such a strong presence in drug research and testing, relates in part to political agendas and priorities.

Political Agenda-setting and Priorities

Follow the money train and either get onboard or derail it. You can do this with your vote.

What role do you think government should have in health? Should government provide health care? Should government use society's resources to fund medical research? What "strings" should they attach? Should there be evidence of efforts to bring the benefit back to the taxpayers? Do political leaders really have anything to do with medical research? The fact is that many nations do have what's called "universal health care." These include Australia, Spain, Japan, Canada, the UK, and France. These government sponsored systems have many limits on them, including the fact that they usually exclude dental, vision, and hearing, as well as medical services not identified as clinically necessary. These services can be purchased with private insurance. But this illustrates the path to health discussed in Chapter 2. It's "normal" to treat health as many parts and neglect the whole. Still, models around the world are showing positive effects for government sponsored health care. Spain achieved lower infant mortality rates than the US or Britain by the early 1970s with care being delivered through its decentralized system of 17 autonomous communities.[207] And France, which was named in 2000 by WHO as having the best health system in the world, continues to have an increase in the population's average life expectancy each year since providing universal access to treatment.[208]

Political priorities also have measurable effects on what medical research gets funded, in turn affecting the health and welfare of citizens. Government is one of the largest sponsors of medical research. Yet, we don't often hear political candidates make statements about what priorities they will set for the nation's medical research. As suggested in the photos in Figure 7.1, tens of thousands of us are showing up for political rallies, but we're often not sure what we expect to hear once we're there. Across the world, asking the question, "What are your medical research priorities?" warrants making it onto the agenda in

Figure 7.1 20,000 show up at Penn State to hear the agenda of a US presidential candidate.

debates and in town hall meetings and in media interviews and public rallies. But it seldom does.

Access to opportunities to participate in medical research and the benefits it accrues says a lot about a society's political agendas and priorities as well. Worldwide, socioeconomic status contributes to health disparities. In turn, these create medical research disparities based on a lack of representation.[209] First, people with less income often make fewer visits to the doctor, even within societies with some form of universal health care. So they have fewer opportunities to be recruited to clinical trials. Second, people with less income may have less ability to meet inclusion criteria that might include following specific diet and lifestyle guidelines that they can't afford.

Political agendas and priorities also form the boundaries for what's "legal" and "ethical" as defined by policies and regulations. They set standards for research, including informed consent and recruitment. There are real abuses of the consent process, both past and present, that cause us to distrust medical research and researchers. In the US, the specter of the historical Tuskegee experiment, as discussed in Chapter 2, begun when there was no treatment for syphilis but continued well past the period when treatment was available, form beliefs about medical research.[210] Participants were told they had "bad blood" while doctors made sure that the men went without treatment, resulting in morbidity and mortality for the men, their wives, and their children. We also have some historical reference in textbooks and World War II movies to the disfiguring and often deadly experiments performed on Nazi prisoners. Additionally, the misuse of prisoners for research purposes in penal systems throughout the world has contributed to our distaste for the conduct of medical research.

In the US, strict legislation stopped the recruitment of prisoners into clinical trials in the late 1970s.[211] In the early twenty-first century, arguments emerged to remove restrictions on the use of prisoners in the US for clinical trials, asserting the right of prisoners to have a choice to make this personal commitment to the goals of science. The Institute of Medicine (IOM) examined the evidence of past abuse and present need, and offered some recommendations.[212] Several precautions were noted in the context of recommending that prisoners once again be recruited to trials but only with strict governance of ethical conduct and care. It seems likely that prisoners will be recruited for a disproportionate number of Phase I trials. Why? Because these studies are conducted on healthy volunteers who are paid to participate and mostly supervised in clinical settings. It becomes difficult to imagine who *volunteers* for such research. The unemployed? We've seen this played out in "humorous" fashion in such movies as *Fun with Dick and Jane* released in 2005. For the prison population, an opportunity to be separated from the general prison population, be fed well to meet a study's protocols, and be cared for medically while participating may indeed form reasons to consent. Might a prisoner be making a choice to participate to gain these "benefits?" Couldn't societies do a better job of publicizing trials, explaining costs and benefits, and recruiting participants?

Media reports continue to keep us appraised of failures to inform us of our unwitting participation in medical research. In the US, during the spring of 2008, debate highlighted the fact that people received artificial blood products when they had no choice about consenting to do so.[213] For some years, efforts to develop a product that can substitute for having *no* blood in emergency situations has motivated researchers to develop blood products. As part of the evolution to market, blood products went into trials in communities that "consented" via *governing* representatives to be involved through delivery of emergency services. Results of use have shown that products nearly triple the risk for heart attacks when compared to blood.[214] Communities participating were not told about all the known risks.

My dad had open heart surgery "off-pump" in 2000, a development that emerged in the last half of the 1990s but was being debated even as he had the surgery. The term "off-pump" refers to maintaining a beating heart during the operation. "On-pump" relies on a heart-lung machine to maintain blood circulation during surgery. What is described as "the world's largest cardiac surgery clinical trial" began in 2008 with the goal of recruiting 4,700 patients to see what differences in outcomes occur using on-pump versus off-pump techniques.[215] The study is projected to last more than seven years and involve 16 countries. It's being led by a Canadian research team. I suspect that there are informed consent nightmares coming online with the study, not just relating to 16 different countries but also for every hospital or clinic where the study may recruit. Why? Can't we form some standards? As with food labeling discussed in Chapter 6, such redundancies have tremendous financial costs linked to them. And they create a pathway to public distrust as well. It's not always political agendas that sway disputes about what research to fund, however. Some topics are sidelined based on where a society "draws the line" with regard to the meaning of the "sanctity of life," which is often defined by religious agendas and priorities.

Religious Agendas and Priorities

Have an advance directive. Make copies of it. Let your loved ones know what it says and where it is.

When it comes to conducting medical research and providing health care, two questions may lead to quite different answers. "Can it be done?" versus "Should it be done?" Religious agendas and priorities define health in terms of institutional and individual *moral* obligations. Faith-based organizations influence pursuit of medical science by taking positions on issues such as cloning or stem cell research from the view of morality. Religious agendas and priorities often raise questions and challenge the "science." The meaning of the "sanctity of life" in these debates, however, adapts to the values and the science of a given point in time. Organ transplantation, for example, has gone from being a rare event, associated with *no* science, Dr. Christiaan Barnard, and media images of research labs and apes, to being "expected" as an option in any respectable cardiology unit. As science about organ donation has become more commonplace, efforts to get us to donate our organs include connecting the pledge to do so to an assertion of our generosity. Organ donation honors rather than violates the sanctity of life. We in our own death can extend the life or lives of others through our "gift."

Religious agendas and priorities may help to keep concern about profiteering in the public views and debates. Making a profit from any innovative practice or therapy moves it out of the realm of acceptability within religious agendas. Thus, it's still not "acceptable," for example, to *sell* human organs. Such a practice falls over the line regarding the sanctity of life. But the line is a little fuzzy, as efforts to produce and reproduce human parts – including skin, the largest organ of the body – are ongoing. In part, this can be argued to be an altruistic pursuit rather than a pursuit for profit. The need for organs far outdistances the supply. Those with lower socioeconomic status will be disadvantaged in an environment with such a limited supply. But the need also tempts some to become an underground supply chain, disadvantaging poorer people who may sell an organ, such as a kidney, to pay for food and utilities. The fact that research is ongoing to try to create human organs is a sign about decisions to allocate resources for medical research in this area. And so it goes, sometimes making it difficult for us to punctuate the reality and understand where profit motives end and human motives begin.

Religious priorities suggest that some types of care or counseling won't be available based on "conscience clauses."[216] Use of these clauses in institutions or by individuals asserts their right to refuse to provide services due to personal beliefs or values. In a Catholic hospital, these may, for example, relate to counseling about birth control or refusal to fill prescriptions for birth control. Religious agendas also frequently define when and how we stop efforts to prolong life. "End-of-life decision-making" versus "assisted suicide" may be conversations about the same issue but the ways the discussions are framed convey different views about actions taken. The former opens a space for comprehension and comparison of alternatives, while the latter presumes a violation of values.[217] These debates occur across the world with some countries, such as Switzerland, the Netherlands, and Belgium, decriminalizing assisted suicide.[218]

Sometimes it all gets a bit confusing for us and so we procrastinate in having discussions with our families about end-of-life decisions or making a living will, with procrastination itself a decision that will, once more, affect us. Whether or not to have such a document is a decision for each individual to make, which of necessity is influenced by religious faith. In the US, a woman named Teri Schiavo[219] died at about the same time as Pope John Paul II. The Pope didn't choose to be placed on life-sustaining medical support systems but expressed support for Teri Schiavo's parents to keep her on such equipment. The difference between being "placed on" versus "removed from" support systems are decisions with religious dimensions which can be perplexing. If humans have greater latitude in their own deaths, might advertisers sell packages for "last suppers" and "final destination" trips? The 1973 movie, *Soylent Green*, depicts such a world in 2022, with severe environmental degradation leading to massive societal problems and sanctioned suicide as the norm.

One of the best ways to ward off abuses of whatever government policies and profit motives exist is to let someone know about our end-of-life desires, especially when it involves them so that they can work to carry out our wishes. In France, for example, among 426 elderly patients 70 years of age or older, 73 percent designated a family member as a surrogate. Another 28 percent identified a second surrogate, usually a family physician.[220] These decisions and our options emerge not only out of political and religious agendas and priorities, but may be guided by the interests of medical associations or others representing health care.

Medical Associations and Lobbyists

Support efforts to increase the use of telemedicine.

Who else funds medical research to form knowledge about health? Who else guides decisions about how health care will be delivered and paid for? Not surprisingly, it's often the organizations representing the diverse health care and medical workforce. Many of us belong to an organization affiliated with the work that we do. We belong because it's nice to vent to others who not only know what we're talking about but have some ideas about how to handle the good, the bad, and the ugly. We belong because it's nice not to have to translate everything we do talk about into language that doesn't include any of our "jargon." We belong because it provides points for comparison relating to how much we're paid, what expectations go along with the work that we do, and when to try to remedy injustice in either realm. Not surprisingly, doctors, nurses, pharmacists, and most other groups that form the field of medicine in its broadest sense also have organizations that they belong to for some of these very same reasons.

Public health and medical associations promote solidarity within professions, creating identities. Medical research is often funded by these organizations. Such research is likely to address how the sponsoring group might do their job better. But that grants a very wide latitude for defining the focus of research questions. So, for example, I've been an advisor on a grant funded by the National Society of Genetic Counselors awarded to a genetic counselor. She wants to develop a tool to guide communicating with patients based on their expectations for the session. I've been an investigator on a grant funded by the American Association of Medical Colleges. It aimed to understand how the use of geographic information systems (GIS) – a computer-based technology tool with unique capacity to enrich understanding of disease models via representations in maps – is shaping cancer research and policies. The focus, as might be expected by the name of the funder, was on what needs exist for training to understand and use these tools.

Industries connected to delivering health and medical care form identities as well – the medical device industry, the pharmaceutical industry, the vaccine industry – as described in Chapter 1. They, too, frequently have organizations that represent them. These form around the core profit motive for each and aim to have representation for "the industry" as a whole. Beyond government-sponsored medical research, industry-funded medical research comprises a very large resource base for support. Pharmaceutical companies, for example, sometimes are criticized for the huge sums of monies put into this endeavor. Yet, we wouldn't think of criticizing IBM for having a Research and Development Division. As long as pharmaceutical companies must adhere to the regulations laid down for such studies, why wouldn't we want and even expect them to put some of their profit back into such pursuits?

Medical associations and industries define codes of behavior for their professions and businesses. They take positions on DTC advertising, for example.[221] They form criteria for behavior that may extend, conflict with, or support the regulatory approach advanced by government. They create rules for entry, including education requirements. Much of the budget and efforts for national and local organizations are spent on deciding medical care standards, including ethics and education. Medical associations also advance requirements for licensing. These may, by turn, create inequities in research and care in the US.

The use of telecommunications technologies and electronic information enable long-distance clinical health care throughout the world for tele health care, tele follow-up care, and distant medical education. For example, studies have shown that best results for procedures such as organ transplant are achieved with lifetime follow-up.[222] This can be achieved through use of telemedicine in which a transplant tertiary expert and a local physician consult with a patient. Globally, efforts to support licensure portability programs are being studied. The UK's Telemedicine Association, for example, envisions a paradigmatic shift in health care during the twenty-first century that will require international medical licensing. The present system, however, creates time-consuming and costly constraints to telemedicine. Credentialing is based on passing a given governing body's licensing exam – a state within the US or a province within Canada, for example. Efforts to be licensed in more than one area take time and are often financially burdensome. Concerns have been expressed about the need to assure the quality of experts providing care. Both sides of this issue have presented their case through representation, often by lobbyists, to governing bodies.

Lobbying is a strategic endeavor by individuals and organizations to influence the opinions of government representatives. Every one of the medical associations and industries linked to health care is likely to have someone who acts as a liaison between their group and the political body governing their country. In a world that is overwhelmed by information, someone has to break it down and make it consumable. We shouldn't expect it to be otherwise. But it's the accountability that needs to have public transparency. In the UK, for example, the public, various medical professional societies, businesses, and commercial organizations all have been identified in efforts to lobby Parliament on behalf of citizens' health.[223] Similar activities go on in the US, with lobbyists who represent health insurance companies added to the mix.

One notable difference between the UK and the US relating to lobbying activities is that the Lobbying Disclosure Act in the US[224] requires reports of monies spent. In 2000, for example, health care lobbying totaled $237 million. That was 15 percent of all lobbying expenditures at the national level that year and involved 1,192 organizations. Pharmaceutical and health product lobbyists spent $96 million – nearly one third of the total amount spent. Physicians and other health professionals spent another $46 million, so that combined with the drugs and product efforts, comprised more than half of the lobbying activity. Patient advocacy and public health organizations added another $12 million.[225] Such advocacy efforts add a final voice in the politics of what medical research to fund.

Patient Advocacy

Find out what advocacy groups represent your health conditions. Get involved.

Does anyone *really* care or want to know what we think? As a matter of fact, they often do. And, as difficult as it is to recruit participants to medical research, it's sometimes equally challenging to get input to the process. Medical associations, the industry groups, and their lobbyists all come to us – the "patients" or "consumers." They seek our input. We have bi-directional influence opportunities in this regard, if we choose to get involved. They seek us out to give feedback, sit on boards, review grant proposals, and offer ideas about research that needs to be done, products that would be helpful, services that are lacking, and our experiences.

In the US, the National Cancer Institute seeks patient advocates as reviewers on the panels that review grants.[226] The person who functions in this role is asked to provide his or her view as a survivor regarding the value of a proposal. Having sat at review tables with advocates, I know that their experience can change the tone about an application. Something that might not meet the "gold standard" for research design but is highly regarded by the advocate will be carefully discussed. The advocate may see its potential to ease the burden of following a medication or other health regimen, improve quality of life through the reduction of pain, or increase marital satisfaction by increasing understanding of a role to be played by marriage partners having the skills to assist with cancer treatment decisions. This makes the rest of the reviewers sit up and take notice. Participating matters.

Too often, we don't know about these opportunities. When we do know, we may feel too intimidated to get involved. My own introduction to the importance of advocacy came in the 1990s as part of a project involving migrant farmworkers, as pictured in Figure 7.2. The project aims focused on cancer prevention. The program manager for cancer control activities in the state of Georgia in the US, the woman I introduced at the end of Chapter 5, included me in these efforts which were disseminated mostly through migrant health clinics.[227]

Patient advocacy groups don't just wait to be asked for their views. They are activists in efforts to gain representation in policy. As a result they look for opportunities to work with medical associations, industry, and lobbyists. They create such opportunities where they don't exist. In the UK, for example, the National Health Services Centre for Involvement[228] is a patient and public resource centre that works with patient and public advocates, providing relevant issue information. Politics and patient advocacy interact in efforts such as those of the director of the NIH in the US in seeking people to become members of the Council of Public Representatives.[229] Members may be asked, for

Figure 7.2 From the author's fieldwork scrapbook: migrant farmworkers at work.

example, to give advice on how to build public trust in the research process. The influencers reach toward us to get this input. In this day and age, nearly any organization has a homepage on the internet. Visiting it will likely reveal opportunities to be involved.

Many organizations relating to health and health care post reports and documents online for public review and seek input before finalizing the texts. As part of the Cochrane Collaboration, CCNet, or the Cochrane Consumer Network, for example, participants give input into the development of Cochrane reviews of evidence in health care.[230] Once an organization says it will seek and apply public feedback, our lack of participation may lead them to reach out to their staff, who reach out to those they know and in a snowball fashion, advocates are found. They may be great but they may also be overused or underrepresentative. With our awareness, however, we can open their pool to a broader sample to choose from by tossing our name and our interest into the pool. It takes time. Time is a limited resource. But somehow and some way, each one of us can get involved. If we find that they don't select us, and we don't think they're hitting the mark, so to speak, we have a chance to influence them in a different direction. We can contact them and provide our unsolicited feedback. Most organization internet home pages offer a way to contact them and that's an open invitation to be involved. If they still don't listen, we have other options that include strategically giving our story to the media.

Without an invitation to do so, many of us are organizing into advocacy groups around living with a particular disease or being the families of those affected and not waiting for those in authority to ask. Advocacy skills include the ability to communicate our needs and to nego- tiate with employers, insurers, and health care providers, as well as to talk to politicians.[231] Advocacy efforts are undertaken on behalf of our own or a loved one's well-being. And these efforts usually pay off for us. AIDS patients' experiences with and involvement in advocacy efforts, for example, contribute to a greater likelihood of getting the information they need to make informed decisions.[232] We're using our power to act and voice our views across many types of disease and many situations affecting our health.

Not surprisingly, size of patient representative organizations is posi- tively related to being involved with advocacy.[233] The more of us there are with a single aim or intention, the more resources we'll have to draw on to develop position statements and make sure they reach our intended audiences. But the more likely it will also be that we'll need money to achieve our goals. Pharmaceutical companies and medical device industries and government all fund advocacy efforts. It behooves us to keep track of who may be providing financial support for an advo- cacy group we join. While we may be a group that has been ignored by drug companies or believe that they should spend research dollars on finding therapies for us, what we don't want to discover is that our group is just another way for the company to lobby politicians to put dollars toward a single way of addressing an issue.

Public health professionals and practitioners may undertake advocacy efforts as well. Injury prevention faculty from Johns Hopkins became a source of information to support the passage of a law in Maryland to limit the availability of certain types of handguns.[234] While such organizations as the police, the medical community, and many civic groups favored passage of the law, they lacked data about the public health problem related to the issue. The public health experts provided data contributing to the ability to refute arguments raised by the pro-gun groups. As pro-gun groups continued to debate the legitimacy of these laws, judicial decisions in the US led some cities to repeal them. That doesn't end the efforts of citizens on the side of efforts to limit access to guns, and it doesn't end the role of advocates within public health and medical associations from supporting these efforts.

Nonprofit organizations also may form to advocate for members, with rights as social welfare organizations to engage in nearly unlimited lobbying with lawmakers, arguing for a position on relevant legislation.[235]

The National Psoriasis Foundation, for example, functioning as a patient advocacy organization with lobbying and advocacy efforts contributed to the development of a psoriasis gene bank and acceptance of psoriasis therapies by insurers.[236] Successful advocacy thus requires use of media in combination with community organizing to advance public health policies by targeting policy-makers, organizations, and legislative bodies.[237] Both directly and indirectly, the results will relate to who participates in medical research and who has access to the care derived from research results.

Summing It Up . . .

Medical research guides what doctors say, what news reports, and what products and services will be derived and delivered. In turn, it affects what *we* say. The state of the science tells us something about outcomes of fundamental debates which led to choices about the allocation of tax dollars to some research topics but not others, exploration of drug and treatment therapies in concert with basic science, and translation of evidence into health messages. We thus need to give more attention to how resources for medical research are being allocated.

A look at the roster of initiatives included in the US National Institutes of Health, the United Kingdom's Department of Health, France's Agency of Health Safety of Health Products, and the UK's Medical Research Council affords a sense of how past decisions have been institutionalized. In the US, the topics of cancer, eyes and vision, the human genome, aging, and alcohol abuse are among the named institutes. In the UK, research boards for infections and immunity, molecular and cellular medicine, neurosciences and mental health, and population and systems medicine represent the major divisions of research activities. As a result, the science and evidence in these areas grows, because these institutes have budgets for medical research on these topics. That doesn't mean, however, that the agenda includes anyone like us or any research to examine therapies considered to be outside the traditional biomedical realm.

The politics of medical research and health care is a personal one. It's told by experiences such as former US Senator Paul Wellstone who heard the stories of citizens about the crippling effects of muscular dystrophy (MD). The media told these stories each year in the US that Jerry Lewis moderated a telethon to raise funds for medical research on MD, revealing the influence of media stories and advocacy efforts. But Senator Wellstone added his direct influence to move MD up the political agenda for medical research in the US. His action got the Muscular Dystrophy Community Awareness, Research, and Education Act passed. In November of 2001, $4.5 million dollars were given for MD research, and the resources have guided the generation of new knowledge.[238] Unless we talk to our elected representatives, join advocacy groups linked to research agendas, and act to be informed and inform others, we may not be represented in medical research or political agendas for health.

What research is funded forms the foundation of scientific evidence we have to communicate about health. It forms the foundation linked to identities that form about health. It guides how individuals and institutions manage health. The knowledge is a type of gate-keeper at the institutional level. Greater understanding about MD, for example, means protocols to guide who receives what care and who will pay for it are debated and emerge where before, without the medical evidence of a need, no resources were allocated for treatment and services. The communication is so integrally involved with how we define health and what options we have, it's recognizable only by intention. While we have developed some skills linked to recognizing advertisers' intent to sell us products, we have *not* turned our efforts toward understanding how decisions are made about which medical research gets funded.

8

An Agenda for the Twenty-first Century: Increase Informed Choice and Consent, or "If I Ran the Circus . . ."

On the coffee table in my family room sits a first edition copy of the Dr. Seuss book, *If I Ran the Circus* (1956). The classic is one of my favorites. I read it to my children and now I read it to my grandchildren. It always makes me smile. There are a couple of themes in it that apply to life generally and communicating about health specifically. One is that we often don't mind all of the fuss and bother in the long run if things work out well. It's the short run that complicates our lives. Second, everyone has an opinion or two about the way the world should be run and how to make things better or worse. When communicating about health, the six questions of primary interest in this book reveal how that happens. We get caught up in the business of deciding whether we are normal, living our lives to the fullest extent we can to reap rewards and avoid punishments, getting care when others seem to agree that it's import- ant, trying to buy products and services to guarantee health, and taking for granted a public health system that regulates safety and quality across many health-linked domains. We listen to the politics of government and our religious groups, and wonder how and why health care gets to be so contentious.

I am a fan of the big picture. I like to place what is happening into a context. I don't like to forget the past or pretend that there are no precedents. This merits comments from undergraduates on teaching evaluations such as, "Our professor sounds like she is giving a political speech sometimes." They don't mean this to flatter me, but I am flattered nonetheless. It reflects the reality that I have introduced them to Gandhi, for example, and had the one student in class whose heri- tage is Indian email to thank me for the lecture. Or I explain how

California's tanning booth legislation made its way onto legislators' dockets and we look at the stories of some of the internet sites where advocacy groups are working to stop indoor tanning salons from being licensed. I like to pose questions for discussion. I don't have all the answers. And I don't pretend to. But I believe in our ability to come up with answers if we talk about it. I have the same opinion about health and health care in the twenty-first century. I've offered throughout the discussion in this book some ideas about how to use the six questions that guide communicating about health to advance each of our personal aims. Here I want to conclude with a few thoughts about informed decision-making to guide our choices and consent in the twenty-first century when communicating about health.

Make "Personalized Medicine" Personal

"Methylenetetrahydrofolate reductase mutation."[239] My doctor wrote it down. "Heterozygous." He was giving me the same news that one of my sisters had received and shared with me. So I already had some idea about what it meant based on her story – which, as we discussed in Chapter 2, often forms our understanding. But I listened carefully to hear what my doctor would tell me and how it compared to what my sister had said. "Heterozygous means you inherited this from just one of your parents. Since you inherited it, you have a chance of passing it on to your own children." High school and college biology and the Punnett square diagram showing possible genetic combinations flashed through my head. Quite a mouthful if I hadn't already been ready for the news.

Without pausing or waiting for my possible or even likely questions, my doctor continued. "Having this version of the gene increases your risk for blood clots and heart disease. It also affects homocysteine levels as it relates to folate."[240] What? Wait a minute. I knew about the blood clots but this was more than my sister had told me. "I'm recommending that you take a super-B complex vitamin. You can get them at any drug store or wherever you buy your aspirin and such." My sister's doctor didn't prescribe a vitamin for her. At least she didn't tell me if he did. "You're also heterozygous for the Factor V Leiden mutation. It, too, increases risk for blood clots.[241] There are things you should and shouldn't do knowing that you have these risk factors. Don't sit on planes or in cars for long periods of time without getting up and moving around. Stay hydrated. Drinking water is important. Really, all of us should pay attention to these things but someone with more risk factors for clotting must be vigilant about these matters. Any questions?" my doctor asked as he shut my chart. Maybe I shook my head but I don't think so. Anyway, before a blink of an eye, my doctor said, "OK, if you think of any, we can talk about it the next time I see you." What? In a year? Are you kidding me? And that's pretty much how the introduction to personalized medicine in the twenty-first century frequently goes. And we often don't think about asking for a referral to a genetic counselor because our doctor doesn't recommend it, and our family or friends don't know that such services are available.[242]

The focus in personalized, also called predictive, medicine[243] emphasizes what role our genetic make-up has for our health. With the completion of the mapping of the human genome, medical research increasingly uses our genetic make-up as a guide to form recommendations about prevention and therapies – but mostly without genetic counseling, without any discussion about heredity and the test results. That's because it's our primary care doctor who's ordering the lab tests and interpreting the results. They're keeping up to date on this almost overwhelming flood of findings from research linking genes to health by attending continuing education programs and conferences, together with reading the piles of journals we often see sitting on their desks and bookshelves as we pass by their offices on the way to examining rooms. And as they have conversations with us about the role of genes for health, new identities may form, blame may shift a bit in our understanding about health and the causes of disease, and we get some idea of how resources for medical research have been allocated of late.

So what do *we* need to know in the twenty-first century when facing personalized medicine at personal and public health levels? First, we should realize that humans all share mostly the same genes, but we may have different versions, or alleles, of the same gene. The version of a gene that is less common is referred to as a mutation. Here's the challenge. Hundreds of genetic mutations have been identified that relate to chronic diseases including diabetes, cancer, and heart disease. The equation relating to these contributors doesn't add up in neat and tidy ways to predict our health status. Just as we considered in Chapter 2, and just as with my diagnosis of *two* genes that increase my risk for forming blood clots, I can't say that I have a 50 percent risk with one and a 100 percent risk because I have two such genes. I can't even say that one increases my risk by 10 percent and the other by 15 percent so that I have a 25 percent greater likelihood of experiencing a blood clot than someone without these factors. It just doesn't work that way.

Second, we should also realize that genetic mutations are "normal." Most of us will have one or more mutations identified in our screening tests in coming years if it hasn't happened already. The language used to describe different gene versions exemplifies the reality that how we talk about health and heritage contributes to forming our sense of self. "Mutation" appears to be an unfortunate label for many of us. Research has shown that the word "mutation" conjures up images of *bad, unhealthy, not normal,* and *undesirable.*[244] An alteration, on the other hand, was perceived as "intended" rather than "unintended" when compared to the other terms. This may foretell the types of expectations forming around genomic health care. We may think that all the medical research is leading to the ability of our doctors to tweak our genes in ways that we *intend* in order to improve our health. Not so.

Third, we should keep in mind that mutations are random events that happen all the time. If a mutation by itself causes no general change in someone's health or actually leads to an improvement in a person's health, it may be passed on. And with time, it may provide a survival advantage in some area. However, while the mutation version of a gene may protect us from some threat to our health, it may also cause a threat to our health. This is true for single gene disorders, such as cystic fibrosis and sickle cell disease which are caused by a defect in one particular gene and have predictable inheritance patterns, as well as genetic versions linked to chronic diseases. The Factor V Leiden mutation I have, for example, not only increases my risk for forming blood clots but also may promote my ability to survive acute respiratory syndrome[245] or severe sepsis when the body is fighting infection.[246] With these basics in mind, the reality we face is that informed decisions about health in the twenty-first century depend upon our awareness that predictive medicine is guiding clinical practice. In other words, personalized medicine is *personal,* as my youngest sister in her story, in Table 8.1, and pictured with her daughter, in Figure 8.1, make clear. Theirs is a success story involving personalized medicine.

Personalized medicine is being applied in many areas and will be a growth industry in the twenty-first century. It may increase our doctors'

Figure 8.1   The author's sister and niece.

ability to manage drug dosages based on our individual characteristics. Pharmacogenomics is the area bringing together the research to link pharmacology, genetics, and genomics.[247] For example, warfarin,[248] often known by its brand name of Coumadin, is an oral anticoagulant medication used by millions worldwide to treat disease linked to the blood's tendency to form clots. Users take this medication as part of a regimen aimed at managing blood clotting risk. When using warfarin, the goal is to manage the blood so that it won't clot too easily but will still clot when necessary. This is a rather intricate balance.

People taking warfarin illustrate why communicating about health matters in all the ways discussed throughout this book and must be a conscious act on all of our parts in the twenty-first-century era of personalized medicine. Based on their own efforts, together with those of their doctors, and support from families and friends, warfarin users follow strict dietary guidelines relating to the blood's ability to clot. Some foods affect the blood's clotting tendencies. Some complementary and alternative therapies interact with warfarin.[249] As discussed in Chapter 2, while use of these has become quite "normal," their effects can be devastating in some cases. Talking about use can help avoid this situation for warfarin users, who also have to be conscientious about avoiding OTC products' "hidden" ingredients that might "add up" and affect the blood's clotting tendencies, a reality all of us face in relation to our prescribed and OTC medication use discussed in Chapter 6.

Warfarin users get their blood tested regularly to ensure that it's neither at risk of forming clots nor at risk of being unable to form clots. The "numbers" they get from their lab reports include the PT, or

Table 8.1 The author's youngest sister's story – a pregnancy facilitated by personalized medicine.

I began a relationship with my future husband in college. We knew of each other in high school, but were never officially introduced until my second year in nursing school. While dating, we enjoyed the outdoors and found plenty of time for activities like hiking, biking, canoeing, and coed softball.

Once we got engaged, we had conversations about out life goals. It was established right away that he would need to stay in our home town to carry on his father's business. That was fine by me, because I had no big ambitions to live anywhere else.

When we discussed our plans for children, we both had a dream of having two. The only question that remained was how long we would wait before we started our family. We both agreed that after one year we should start trying to conceive.

That one year turned into six. During that period, we underwent numerous doctor visits and lots of procedures. It was finally concluded that we had "undiagnosed infertility." This is a term they give people when they are not getting pregnant, but there is no obvious reason for why they are not.

We both knew that two beautiful children were in our future. The question that remained was how these children would come to be in our lives. That is when our hearts were opened to adoption. We adopted our son in 1994. What an amazing time in our lives. The thought of more children never came up again, until our son went to kindergarten. He came home from school that first day and said he wanted a sister.

That is where our quest to get pregnant started up again. I ended up being diagnosed with endometriosis this time around. The physician said he could do surgery and the probability of pregnancy would exist, but he wanted to have the genetic testing to rule out the Factor Leiden V mutation first.

Unfortunately, that ended up being positive. I was sent to a specialist for her advice on whether it would even be safe to get pregnant with a high risk for blood clotting. She felt that the risk would be minimal if I were willing to take it.

I got pregnant in the summer of 2000. We found out about it while Dad was recovering from his open heart surgery. My physician wanted me to see a high risk pregnancy doctor. When I went to him, he wanted to do further testing and found that I had antiphospholipid antibody. This is yet another medical condition that sets the stage for increased coagulation and thus clotting. In pregnant women who have this, the stage is set for blood clot formation in the umbilical cord and miscarriages usually in the second trimester are very common.

Table 8.1   (*cont'd*)

Of course, I am finding this out in my sixth week of pregnancy. The treatment to ensure the best outcome was to start immediately giving myself shots of Heparin in the stomach two times per day and to take Prednisone orally. It was explained to us that if we chose not to do this, it was possible that everything might be OK. However, there was no way of knowing until it was too late. Treatment needed to be started in 48 hours to have the best outcome.

We chose to take the medicine and today we have a beautiful daughter, Caity Marie. So, for me personalized medicine meant acquiring all the health information possible, having the correct interpretation of that data, and then being able to make my own decisions about the findings. In this case it meant a nearly full-term pregnancy where before it didn't seem possible.

Karen Wiser, an Intensive Care Nurse until Caity was born and now fulltime mom who works as a volunteer in her children's school

---

prothrombin time, and INR, the international normalized ratio.[250] A standard reference range, as discussed in Chapter 2, should not be used to interpret the meaning of the numbers. Factors such as the patient's age and gender, together with the testing method, affect the meaning of the numbers. The overall goal is to determine how long blood is taking to form a clot. How often the blood gets tested depends upon how stable it is in the ability to clot within a normal reference range. Warfarin users, thus, must be careful and persistent in keeping track of their "numbers," following the suggestions discussed in Chapter 2, such as paying attention to the reference ranges used by labs to report results.

The effort to keep the right balance between blood that is neither too thick nor too thin, blood that doesn't form dangerous clots but also has the ability to clot when necessary, challenges patients and their doctors. In this era of personalized medicine, medical research has identified some genes that affect how a patient responds to warfarin. This means that testing for a small number of genes could improve patient care by identifying the right dosage to promote optimum response.[251] What could be wrong with that? Here is where personalized medicine gets a little tricky. First, if genes affect warfarin response, might they also affect how alternative therapies respond in any given person's body? As discussed throughout the book, far fewer resources have been devoted to research on complementary and alternative treatments. We know far less about their effects. But we know that they have effects. We don't want to lose sight of that reality in this era of personalized medicine.

Second, to reap any benefits linked to a role for genes in predicting warfarin response will require developing and using new tests. As discussed throughout this book, that takes a lot of resources both in terms of time and money, and, of course, the people whose lives would be devoted to the activity. As consumers and taxpayers, we need to assess these costs to the entire medical system and be confident that they are worth our investment. Can it save money for the entire system to test the millions of patients for these genes and base prescribing on the results? Based on the factors that relate to interpreting each patient's results, how much less often will patients have their blood tested? We don't want to lose sight of these questions. That's what will guide informed decisions about personalized medicine. These questions will be asked time and again for countless drug therapies in the coming years as enthusiasm for pharmacogenomics continues to grow.

Not surprisingly, as discussed in Chapter 6, personalizing therapies is crossing multiple domains beyond the use of medications. These include nutritional realms. The discipline of nutrigenomics focuses on how nutrients and genes interact at the molecular level.[252] Remember my own doctor's advice to start taking an OTC super B complex vitamin based on the finding that I had a particular version of one gene linked to blood folate. As seen with my diagnosis, genes can contribute to differences in how our body uses some nutrients that are vital to well-being – like folate. A simple enough action – taking a B vitamin. I do it because it's affordable and easy and doesn't change the routine of my entire household to accommodate my nutritional needs. The research connecting genes and nutrition may help to move the study of dietary supplements from a realm of complementary and alternative therapies, as discussed in Chapter 2, to clinical treatments. This will be based on completion of clinical trials, as discussed in Chapter 7. Online sites have already jumped to the marketing angle, offering analysis of our DNA and advice on what foods to eat and avoid – based on our genetic makeup. The profit motive forms their underlying incentive. There's *no* regulation of these activities to protect consumers. In light of our discussion in Chapter 6, it shouldn't be too surprising to find the cosmetics industry is also poised to leverage the science linking outcomes to genes in personal ways as well. Cosmegenomics relates to how genes interact with functional foods to affect skin and anti-aging, for example. This, too, will contribute to the rise and likely the fall of many industries in the coming years. It will also affect choices we make about our own health.

Genetic variations have also been found which relate to how our personal behaviors and lifestyles relate to genes. Some gene versions link to how alcohol metabolizes in our bodies. Others may increase our motivation to use drugs[253] or smoke.[254] Knowing that we have a gene or genes that appear to make us have a tendency to drink, take drugs, or smoke and lead us to have health problems in these areas is billed as a way to motivate us to avoid actions in these areas. But it might not. We might just become fatalistic about our health, as discussed in Chapter 4, if we have the genes, or, be overly optimistic if we don't have these genes. In the meantime, lots of resources get devoted to supporting the research, tests have to be developed to identify the gene versions, and we may shift our sense of responsibility in this area. If the same resources allocated for research to translate findings that genes link to behavioral predispositions were instead spent on efforts to support prevention, screening, and treatment, might all of us benefit? Remember that personalized medicine is *personal*, whether we have a gene linked to disease named or not. It's costing us and society tremendous resources, framing how we think about our identities related to health, and contributing to how we think about responsibility for health. In reality, the best *genetic* test is often family history. But that requires us to both know and tell.

Be Timely in the Telling

The mapping of the human genome and discoveries relating health conditions such as blood clotting risk to multiple genes and their variants are changing communication about health in and out of the clinic. The changes may be subtle if you're not listening for the queries that reflect these differences or for the public prompts to "know your family history" – a direct reference to our biological kin. For some years, doctors have known that one of the most useful kinds of information we can give them is our family health history. They've known this based on the immense database from medical research that links our family history to cancer, heart disease, diabetes, and other chronic conditions. Family history is so important because it includes *not only* the genetic component of health status but also the parts relating to where we live, what we eat, stressors linked to socioeconomic issues, and all the interactions among these. While we've been asked about family history at medical appointments in the past, a greater emphasis has begun to be placed on these questions and our answers. Unfortunately, most of us don't know the answers.

It's not unusual to be unaware of family health history. Doctors often try to collect this information but may not be able to make recommendations based on it because we don't do our part by knowing.[255] Communication about genes and health doesn't offer us the option of getting rid of our genes to control health. But it may motivate us to talk to our doctor about whether we should be tested. Research has, for example, linked one version of a gene to an increased likelihood of having melanoma.[256] If we have melanoma in our family, we might ask our doctor to test us for the gene. If a test is available and we learn that we have the gene, we may be eligible for more frequent clinical screenings for melanoma. We may be more personally vigilant in keeping track of changes on our skin. If we have melanoma in our family and we don't have the gene linked to an increased incidence for the disease, other variables relating to our family history may still put us at increased risk – where we have lived and our sun exposure, for example, as well as where we have worked. These bits of information about ourselves may guide our doctors' decisions about recommendations for screenings as well.

Knowing our own history may save us from countless costly medical tests and lead to more accurate diagnoses because we can tell our doctor things that may only be hinted at from reading the results of lab studies. Blood work in particular may suggest numerous possible paths to explain results that lie outside the "normal" reference range. Timeliness of information about our family health history may affect decision-making about therapies, including medications. In our family, we had discussed our family history for blood clotting which contributed to a decision about the use of a blood-thinning medication before and after my father's bypass surgery. Family history forms a valid guide to indicate when genetic testing for the genes being identified as links to predicting chronic conditions should be conducted. We couldn't have made these informed choices in my family without my sister sharing with us her diagnosis linked to genetic mutations and increased risk for forming blood clots. She told our parents and all of her siblings, including me. Her doctor had advised her to tell us about her status and that we should be tested. That, however, was the limit of the *counseling* he offered.

We may avoid talking about health history with our biological families because the literal "blood ties" that link us together may perpetuate "blame" for disease causation.[257] In theory, no single family member "owns" family health history information. Every member could potentially share certain genetic traits, links, or diseases. In a world where differences may disadvantage us for jobs or how we are viewed by society and in personal relationships, knowing that we have genetic factors linked to disease may seem to offer more risks than benefits. In my family, we all followed my sister's doctor's advice to be tested except for my brother who has still not been tested. He is concerned that somehow a positive diagnosis would or could be used to discriminate against him. In this era of naming genes in health, he's not alone.[258] As a result, in the US, the Genetic Information Nondiscrimination Act was signed into law by President G. W. Bush in 2008. It states that an increased genetic risk for a disease or a family history for the same disease cannot be used to refuse coverage or raise premiums. Ironically, it fails to protect someone who may find a condition in a screening that should merit supervision.[259] These are the kinds of challenges we will face as we move ahead in the twenty-first century in our efforts to be informed in our health decisions. One step forward and sometimes two steps back.

My sister who had the original diagnosis also had both of her children tested and found that her son did not have the mutations but her daughter did. I recommended that my adult children be tested, and as you already know my daughter did, testing negative for the mutations I have. That, however, did not mean she could not develop blood clots from the use of birth control pills – which she did as described in Chapter 2. My son, pictured with my granddaughter in Figure 8.2, has not been tested. Because my daughter-in-law knew my status, she had my granddaughter tested. She did not inherit the genetic tendencies I inherited for blood clotting risk. That doesn't mean my son didn't inherit them, as he, too, would be heterozygous – with me as the parent who could pass the conditions on to him while his father would not. He thus would not necessarily pass them on to his children – even if he has them. But in an environment where much uncertainty yet exists relating to benefits of knowing, he chooses not to know.

In this era when awareness of our family history can prevent needless genetic testing, too little has been done to guide our efforts in this

Figure 8.2 The author's son at age 30 and her first grandchild at age $3^1/2$: he hadn't been tested for Factor V Leiden mutation and she had with a negative result.

regard. It's not enough to tell us to know our family health history. What does that mean? What, why, when, and where all enter into the mix and, in very little time, it's simply too much information even if we are interested in learning such content about our family members. In the US, the Surgeon General launched a campaign in 2004 to get us talking about health histories in our families. Table 8.2 includes some of the questions that the campaign recommends we talk about related to health in our families. With such information, we may be better able to talk with our doctors and contribute to their informed recommendations for our care.

As suggested in Table 8.2, at minimum, when possible, we should know whether our parents, grandparents, aunts or uncles, as well as siblings had cancer, diabetes, or heart disease. We should also know whether they have had a blood clot, stroke, or heart attack. If they had cancer, what type? If they had any of these major diseases or conditions, how old were they when they were diagnosed? And what was the end result of the diagnosis? Did treatment work? Yes? What kind of treatment? Medication? What kind? If treatment didn't work, what was it that did not work? Did the relative die from the disease? If yes, at what age? These prompts form one strategy for guiding our ability to make informed choices and give informed consent when presented with options for genetic testing linked to our health status and therapies. Sounds impossible? Too personal? Only the "old folks" talk about these things? Think again. A passion for family history and genealogy forms the foundation for many thriving industries worldwide – many now being tied to analyses of our DNA. Our health history is another part of the story.

As discussed in Chapter 4, we are often managing our impressions to the detriment of getting health care. One of the obvious challenges

Table 8.2   US Surgeon General's Family History Initiative: National Public Health Campaign

1 Know your personal history for heart disease, stroke, diabetes, colon cancer, breast cancer, and ovarian cancer, including age of diagnosis if relevant.
2 Know the history for these same six conditions for your biological mother and her parents, your father and his parents. Again, know age at diagnosis if any of the six relatives have any of the six conditions. If any of the six are dead, what was their age at the time of death and what was the cause of death?
3 Is there a personal or family history of any other disease or condition (e.g., blood clots)?

Source: US Surgeon General's Family History Initiative. Retrieved from www.hhs.gov/familyhistory/, on 9/25/2008.

linked to telling us to know our family health history is that we don't and won't want to talk about health in our families because we are managing our impressions and theirs. Also, because we don't want to transgress on their time and resources, we limit these discussions. Add to this those situations in which families are estranged and members don't even know where one another lives, let alone talk with each other about health. In these cases, the advice to "know your family health history" becomes difficult if not impossible to follow.

For years, I have given as one option for a semester project in my undergraduate classroom the choice to interview family members and learn about their health histories. I am always confronted with situations in which family dynamics are strained or divorce has created barriers to access to family or both. I remind students that they have other options for their semester project. And I also tell them that students in the past who have faced a similar situation have sometimes found that talking about health histories is a *neutral* zone. It opens a space for conversation. It may not be anything more than a question and answer session, often by email even. But family is usually interested in helping their students in college to earn a good grade. And that can sometimes lead to more. At minimum, they gain some insights about health histories.

I also emphasize that "knowing your health history" is supposed to be a way to integrate the many dimensions of lives into the health experience. That includes where we've lived, our diets, and other contributors to health that genes alone will not explain. Because this is such a vital part of our health history, students who are adopted have the option to focus on this part of the health equation if it is the information to which they have access. And we discuss adoptees' advocacy efforts to gain access to their biological parents' health histories. We conclude with a discussion of diasporic families, where family members are scattered worldwide while maintaining some link to a specific nation. Vietnamese families, for example, have migrated to the US, France, China, Australia, and Canada – to name just a few of the countries where they went to escape political persecution, while often leaving kin behind. Not that we need to become obsessed with knowing these things. Too much focus on the myriad of ways that health can be negatively affected has contributed to a group that doctors refer to as the "worried well,"[260] who spend too much time and energy on trying to be healthy across every domain.

It's important for our medical records, however they are stored – paper or paperless – to include the fact that a doctor talked to us about specific family health history information. In efforts to increase our informed decisions, even when we don't know family history, it should still be recorded that we were asked and that the information was unobtainable at that visit. We and our doctors should follow up at the next visit to fill in missing information. An innovative use of technology might include having our health care organizations prompt us about what we may need to find out shortly before we go to an appointment. This may include finding out where we lived as a toddler and what our parents did for a living, suggesting possible exposures. These sorts of insights will help build understanding of how genes and environments interact. Email reminders or letters to our homes may provide a way of letting us know what the doctor will ask about family history at the appointment. Both participants in the medical history-taking component must thus do their part to follow through on public efforts to promote both knowing and telling.

Fill in the Blanks

Medical science discovers generalities and probabilities, describes risks and trade-offs, and may make advice and techniques accessible. As discussed in Chapter 6, many of us learn about scientific discoveries through the news and entertainment media. We share the information with others or act upon the information in hopes of benefiting our health. Research on human genes, like that done as part of the Human Genome Project, is no different. It was debated in scientific, political, religious, and personal realms. Reports about these conversations appeared in newspapers and scientific journals. Sometimes, the debates themselves were aired on TV and had broad public audiences. Scientific understanding of the genome was presented as a path toward disease prevention. This generated great enthusiasm and opened the flood gates to resources in much the same manner as racing to land on the moon did.

The first broad media coverage about genes during the era of the Human Genome Project was stories about breast cancer and the BRCA1 and BRCA2 mutations.[261] Many women sought testing for genetic contributors to breast cancer in the wake of media reports about breast cancer and genes when they had no family history to suggest the presence of a gene related to increased susceptibility.[262] In other words, news stories about a "breast cancer gene" contributed to women's beliefs about the role of genes in disease processes, but not always accurately.[263] Before the era of genomic health care, communication about *one* gene predicting the likelihood of inheriting *one* disease was fraught with complexities. When someone is tested for a gene relating to cystic fibrosis or sickle cell disease, for example, the genetic test result provides enough information to guide communication about the likelihood that he/she will inherit or carry the condition. Genetic counseling in situations where someone is a carrier of a gene relating to these single gene conditions will relate to many decisions relating to important life issues. Who will the carrier tell about the condition, an invisible one, and when? How will it affect decisions about having children?

Multiple genetic contributors to a health condition multiply the complexity relating to communication about genes and health. Before ever getting such a test, we should consider what we expect to happen based on the results. Do we expect to prevent disease? Do we expect to detect disease early? Do we expect to predict whether our children will inherit susceptibility for a particular condition? Just because we can test does NOT mean that there is any treatment – particularly preventive treatment. A genetic test result gives us, and our family and medical care team, *one* piece of information about our health. Remember, our lifestyles, our occupations, our forms of recreation – these often relate to our health. And while the general population has reported high levels of interest in being tested for genetic predispositions to disease, we also convey little understanding of the implications of test results.[264]

Medical tests are not perfect. A medical test's sensitivity and specificity are important in giving it credibility when priorities for clinical and public health relating to genes and health are made. If a specific test fails to identify a lot of people as having a condition when they actually have it, the test isn't very sensitive in its ability to say who's at risk. If a specific test identifies a lot of people as having a condition when they don't actually have it, it's not good at identifying specifically who is at risk. When medical research finds connections between genes and chronic conditions, investors decide whether developing a test to indicate the gene's presence is worthy of investment, as discussed in Chapter 6. And then tracking how specific and sensitive the test is may take some time and lead to revision.

When we have a genetic test done, we should ask our doctor about the test's sensitivity and specificity. If we are thinking about a test, we want to know that the results will be meaningful for us in making decisions about our health. That begins with our confidence that the test has been done right and reflects our actual health status. If we have a family history of some mutations being diagnosed but our own tests come back negative, we want to feel confident that the results are accurate. If we agreed to testing, it was because we and our doctors planned to use the results to guide decisions about our health. We want them to be decisions based on valid results. Testing is improving, as methods to automate DNA analysis have been designed, providing more accurate results that are easier to use. These include bio-imaging systems such as GeneGnome[265] which automate the process of imaging chemiluminescent samples. As a result, the ability to be accurate in telling a woman that she has BRCA1 or BRCA2 mutations, for example, has been enhanced.

The options relating to genetic testing information, however, mostly do not include replacing, manipulating, or supplementing the genes – gene therapy. Gene therapy is the use of genes to treat or prevent disease. A mutated gene may be replaced with a healthy copy of the gene. A new gene may be introduced into the body to help fight a disease. Or a mutated gene may be inactivated because it isn't functioning. The technique is experimental and being tested for treatment of diseases that have no other cure. Once more, our exposure to the media enters the scene as the phrase "gene therapy" appears in the media and we gain some general sense of its meaning. These options are being aggressively pursued, for example, in research for preventing cystic fibrosis and sickle cell disease. The research has been successful in studies for sickle cell *using mice*, but even here is years away from use as human therapy. So, once more, communication about these matters raises ethical concerns and legal questions, and has social implications, leaving us to fill in the blanks between what we hear in the news, see in entertainment venues, and become aware of through advertising and marketing ventures.

Track Your Health Report
(. . . and Your Credit Report, Too)

Medical identity theft has become a growing problem worldwide.[266] Medical identity theft relates to the unlawful use of information about our personal health to gain access to health care products and services. These services may range from benefits linked to social security to opening new credit card accounts. It requires our awareness of the crime and action to protect ourselves. In the US, 250,000 reported medical identity theft events accounted for about 3 percent of stolen identity cases in 2005. In Canada and the UK, the national insurance numbers of many citizens have been stolen because they carried these numbers in their wallets. Stolen cards are used for fraudulent social security claims or to open bank accounts and get new credit cards.

Some blame access to our information via information technology for a rise in medical identity theft but the evidence doesn't seem to bolster their case. Worldwide, there are vast differences between nations in their use of health information technology. Such technology makes our personal health data accessible to our doctors at the touch of a computer keyboard. In 2006, thousands of primary care physicians in seven countries were surveyed about the use of electronic medical records. Results revealed that 98 percent of doctors in the Netherlands, 92 percent in New Zealand, 89 percent in the United Kingdom, 79 percent in Australia but just 28 percent in the US and 23 percent in Canada used electronic medical records.[267] With the last two being countries where medical identity theft has become a significant problem, fears that it is linked to the use of electronic medical records appear to be unwarranted.

Privacy concerns have been named as one reason for some nations' limited use of electronic medical records. While the risk for us in having our medical records recorded in electronic form presents an opportunity for violations of privacy, not having such records presents in many cases greater opportunity for these violations to occur. Remember the old "telephone" or "grapevine" game that we played as children? The farther down the line a whispered phrase or sentence went, the more distorted it became. Similarly, the more staff, technicians, and other providers who handle a piece of paper or report about our health, the more opportunities to violate our privacy arise, sometimes with no intention; at other times with intent as celebrities and political leaders often complain.

While we often fear the use of computers to store our personal information, computerized systems may actually protect our privacy. They can rapidly transmit content from one caregiver to another in a health care organization, which may span multiple buildings and sites. Thus, rather than having many hands touch documents relating to our health in an effort to move lab reports and charts from one doctor to another, the computer "sees" our data. The security of the information technology system determines who has access. I have experienced both worlds. Living in a rural community where the information age has not yet guided practice, I wasn't happy to have one of my students tell me one day in class that she'd seen some of my lab reports come in and filed them into my chart. By contrast, when living in Atlanta in the 1990s, the health care system I belonged to was organized in a way that the lab technicians entered lab results into my computerized record, and no matter which doctor in the system I saw or which location I received care at, the doctors had access to relevant health information about me. The benefits of computerized records also emerge when a natural disaster has occurred and paper records are destroyed (so long as computerized systems have back-up reserves with content stored in them off-site in safe locations). Still, in an age when identities are stolen via hacking into computer systems, we want to know how our information will be used when it is being collected for these mass data repositories aligned with public health goals.

Tracking the information kept about your health and medical status should be an important priority to avoid inaccuracies. Consider all the entities that use our health information. Individual health care providers, hospitals, other health care organizations, insurers, employers, educational institutions, health departments, environmental departments, welfare and family services, social security, government disability – the list is quite long. The validity associated with your information being part of any number of databases depends upon your point of view. Taking an active interest in understanding how and why such information is collected and used is the first step to making such judgments. Disclosure of health and health care information is often legally permitted to other health care providers, to epidemiologists or researchers, and under a subpoena or court order.

To safeguard our privacy and our identity, both our medical identity and our credit identity, we should review our medical records. It's important to guard any insurance numbers just as Americans are advised to carefully guard social security numbers and Britons are advised to safeguard their national insurance cards. We should request a full copy of health care files from our providers, especially if we suspect something may be amiss. If something is amiss, as with other identity theft, file a police report, correct false information, and keep an eye on your credit report.[268]

In North America, both the US and Canada, MIB – once known as the Medical Information Bureau – is a nonprofit corporation that provides a point-of-contact to check what others may have access to about us and our health. Owned by about 470 insurance companies, MIB works to detect fraud and avoid fraud relating to efforts to get health, disability, critical illness, long-term care, and life insurance.[269] About 15 to 20 out of each 100 insurance applications generate an MIB record. These records come from the member companies. They include our test results for medical conditions, coded in a confidential format. Under the Fair Credit Reporting Act, we have a right to see and correct the information the MIB has about us.

While medical identities are being stolen, we also persist in being woefully unable to communicate about matters that relate to our own medical identification. Beyond family history, what is it that we don't know in the midst of so much information about health? Table 8.3 includes a few important issues. We too frequently don't know the names of our conditions, the treatments that have been recommended – including the names and dosages of drugs. Because we don't know this information, devastating events such as Hurricane Katrina are even more disastrous.

Table 8.3   Medical Identification Information (MII, pronounced '*me*').

1   What is your blood type?
2   What surgeries have you had (and at what age)?
3   What acute illnesses have you had which limited your ability to work and for how long? (e.g., pneumonia)
4   What chronic conditions do you have? (e.g., knee pain, arthritis, . . .)
5   What medications, at what dosage and frequency, do you take? (generic)
6   What side effects have you experienced from surgeries, treatments, or medications?
7   Any known allergies?

Knowing the name of our conditions, and any medication and dosage we use to adapt to that condition could go a long way to reduce the individual medical chaos in these events. Medical identification communication is a crucial component of communicating about health in the twenty-first century.[270]

Stay Out of "The Big Muddy"

For many decades, public health and medicine shared a common aim in the domain of genetics. It was to promote health through the application of knowledge about genes and health. Newborn screening programs, as discussed in Chapter 5, and screening for single gene diseases such as cystic fibrosis and sickle cell disease form a core component of public health in clinical practice. From the late nineteenth century well into the twentieth century, a movement was under way to improve the physical and mental traits of humans, with some efforts directed at benefiting the public's health via elimination of "bad" genes from the human gene pool. Eugenicists of ill repute targeted only certain groups of us for this activity and often relied on unwitting and uninformed "consent" to sterilize women. These activities contributed to the artificial divide between public and clinical health realms in the US.

The twenty-first century presents an opportunity for public health and clinical practice to once more join efforts to benefit the well-being of us all. But it will require leadership. It will require an informed citizenry.

It will require us to "draw the line," so to speak, in ways we never have before. The reality of future benefits for genomics and human health will often depend upon us, our decisions, and our actions right now. We will be solicited to provide our cooperation in giving lifestyle information, family health histories, personal medical information, and biological specimens. Why? So that genetic databanks might be assembled with linkages to the multiple determinants of health. Because such data exist for some groups, some groups have been identified as being at increased risk for having genetic mutations being related to disease. Among these are Ashkenazi Jews for whom the incidence of genetic mutations linked to breast cancer appears to be greater than for the overall population.[271]

A centralized and accessible national repository of biospecimens focused on supporting genetic research has been proposed in the US. The national biospecimen network (NBN)[272] blueprint commissioned by the National Cancer Institute argues for this level of organization for research linking genes to health. Patient advocates and consumers have objected to the NBN's emphasis on researchers' needs to the neglect of informing donors of what little chance there is to reap personal benefits. Barriers to involving the donors more directly include the fact that deidentification of tissues make it difficult to recontact donors. Realistically, the progression of a patient's disease likely makes treatment based on new information gained irrelevant. But no one is talking about that. In the US, the Secretary of Health formed an Advisory Committee on Genetics, Health, and Society (SACGHS).[273] This promotes our ability to give input to the process, as discussed in Chapter 7, acting as advocates for ourselves in ways intended to gain benefits while avoiding discrimination.

As also discussed in Chapter 7, the timeline for bringing new therapies to fruition based on medical research is a very long one. When it comes to asking us to give our literal life blood, it's fair to ask that the goals of genomic research be stated clearly. How individual tissue samples will be used should be known. For while these actions are linked to eventual personalized medicine aims, the initial activities are taking place at the public level, and validated results would be unlikely to be available during the course of a patient's active disease. This, too, should be clearly communicated to those who agree to give such tissue samples. Once more, the reality of representing genetics and health in terms of research and societal benefit as well as personal risk and benefit is a challenge.

Summing It Up . . .

In the twenty-first century, communicating to make informed decisions about health, to give informed consent, and to be informed about our choices requires that we communicate at the margins of medical research and clinical and public health practice. Margins provide a buffer zone between us and a range of experts whose advice we consider when making decisions about our health. Margins also give a space and place to reflect. We have reached a time when medical research supports the interrelation of many factors in our health. Limited personal and societal resources and competing commercial interests, however, suggest it won't always be evident in the services and care we receive.

In this era of personalized medicine, to make informed decisions and give informed consent, we must weigh the realities that having genetic tendencies doesn't mean that one absolutely will experience a health threat linked to a particular gene. Not having the genes doesn't mean one won't experience the threat linked to the gene. When we spend resources developing tests, conducting tests, and telling people they have genes linked to disease, we need to ask, "For what end gain?" The six questions that guide communicating about health discussed in this book reveal that asking the question and getting the answer won't be easy. Partly, that's because three key conversations are going on at the same time in any talk about health, but only one is likely to be explicitly visible. There's what we experience and how our family, friends, and culture shape that. There's what our doctors tell us through any variety of media based on the evidence from medical research. And there's the discussion at a societal level – what political leaders and religious leaders and those who organize to deliver services, products, and care are saying.

While the only talk being spoken in an examination room will be related to our own health status, politics is present in what our doctor talks about. It funded the research forming the evidence on which the doctor can base a diagnosis and treatment. A profit motive is also present. It's the options the doctor has to offer us and our expectations for therapies based on advertising, and the news and entertainment industries. The public good is there. It's the health message which brought to our attention the importance of coming to the doctor. And it's the influence of family, friends, and other doctors who recommended and supported us in making and keeping that appointment. They're all present in the examination room when the doctor asks a question about symptoms or habits. They're all present when we enter the voting booth to elect political leaders. They're all present when we pick up an item at the store and read its label. We cannot respond to a doctor's questions without thinking about them through the lens of what we've heard in our families about health. Our doctors cannot form the questions they ask us or the advice they give without medical research to suggest guidelines for the discussion. Society cannot "own" its value system without owning its role in our health and health care. We thus will better reflect our own goals in this process by *hearing* the voices of all who are present . . . and making our decisions with clarity, intention, and awareness of this reality.

A Final Thought

Information is a perishable commodity,
. . . but the skills to use information in communicating about health are not . . .

References

1 Why Communicating about Health Matters

1 Choi, Y., Choi, S. M., and Rifon, N. (2007, May). "Phantom smokers": The unidentified who do not identify with smokers. A paper presented at the annual meeting of the International Communication Association meeting held in San Francisco, CA, USA.
2 Morten, A., Kohl, M., O'Mahoney, P., and Pelosi, K. (1991). Certified nurse-midwifery care of the postpartum client: A descriptive study. *Journal of Nurse-Midwifery*, 36, 276–288.
3 Li, Q., Kobayashi, M., and Kawada, T. (2008). Relationships between percentage of forest coverage and standardized mortality ratios (SMR) of cancers in all prefectures in Japan. *Open Public Health Journal*, 1, 1–7.
4 Finkelstein, E. A., Ruhm, C. J., and Kosa, K. M. (2005). Economic causes and consequences of obesity. *Annual Review of Public Health*, 26, 239–257.
5 Isshiki, Y., Morimoto, K., Nakajima, M., Maruyama, S., and Takeshita, T. (2002). Increasing obesity among male workers in Japan: 1992–1997. *Environmental Health and Preventive Medicine*, 6, 256–259.
6 Kageyama, Y. (2008, June 8). Japan tackles worker obesity with financial incentives. *The Mercury News*. Retrieved from www.mercurynews.com/nationworld/ci_9520771, on 6/30/2008.
7 Centers for Disease Control and Prevention, *An Ounce of Prevention . . . What Are the Returns?*, 2nd edn (1999, October). Retrieved from www.cdc.gov/epo/prevent.htm, on 9/26/2008.
8 Drewnowski, A., and Specter, S. (2004). Poverty and obesity: Diet quality, energy density, and energy costs. *American Journal of Clinical Nutrition*, 79, 6–16.

9 Glasgow, R. E., Fisher, E. B., Anderson, B. J., LaGreca, A., Marrero, D., Johnson, S. B., Rubin, R. R., and Cox, D. J. (1999). Behavioral science in diabetes: Contributions and opportunities. *Diabetes Care*, 22, 832–843. Glasgow, R. E., Wagner, E. H., Kaplan, R. M., Vinicor, F., Smith, L., and Norman, J. (1999). If diabetes is a public health problem, why not treat it as one? A population-based approach to chronic illness. *Annals of Behavioral Medicine*, 21, 159–170.

10 Thompson, C. L., and Pledger, L. M. (1993). Doctor–patient communication: Is patient knowledge of medical terminology improving? *Health Communication*, 5, 89–97.

11 Jenkins, V., Leach, L., Fallowfield, L., Nicholls, K., and Newsham, A. (2002). Describing randomization: Patients' and the public's preferences compared with clinicians' practice. *British Journal of Cancer*, 87, 854–858.

12 Chapman, K., Abraham, C., Jenkins, V., and Fallowfield, L. (2003). Lay understanding of terms used in cancer consultations. *Psycho-Oncology*, 12, 557–566.

13 Condit, C. M., Condit, D. M., Dubriwny, T., Sefcovic, E., Acosta-Alzura, C., Brown-Givens, S., Dietz, C., and Parrott, R. (2003). Lay understandings of sex/gender and genetics: A methodology that preserves polyvocal coder input. *Sex Roles*, 49, 557–570.

14 Hall, S., Weinman, J., and Marteau, T. M. (2004). The motivating impact of informing women smokers of a link between smoking and cervical cancer: The role of coherence. *Health Psychology*, 23, 419–424.

15 Rowe, P. (2003). Why is rickets resurgent in the USA? *The Lancet*, 357, 1100.

16 Brash, D. E. (1997). Sunlight and the onset of skin cancer. *Trends in Genetics*, 13, 410–414.

17 US Food and Drug Administration (2008). FDA recommends that over-the-counter (OTC) cough and cold products not be used for infants and children under 2 years of age. Public Health Advisory: Nonprescription Cough and Cold Medicine Use in Children. Retrieved from www.fda.gov/Cder/drug/advisory/cough_cold_2008.htm, on 4/22/08.

18 www.cdc.gov/std/hpv/ScreeningTables.pdf.

19 Caspermeyer, J. J., Sylvester, E. J., Drazkowski, J. F., Watson, G. L., and Sirven, J. I. (2006). Evaluation of stigmatizing language and medical errors in neurology coverage by US newspapers. *Mayo Clinical Proceedings*, 81, 300–306.

20 Blendon, R. J., Schoen, C., DesRoches, C., Osborn, R., and Zapert, K. (2003). Common concerns amid diverse systems: Health care experiences in five countries. *Health Affairs*, 22, 106–121.

2 How "Normal" Am I?

21 Montgomery, K. S. (2000). Apgar scores: Examining the long-term significance. *Journal of Perinatal Education*, 9, 5–9.

22 Odd, D. E., Rasmussen, F., Gunnell, D., Lewis, G., and Whitelaw, A. (2007). A cohort study of low Apgar scores and cognitive outcomes. *Archives of Disease in Childhood – Fetal and Neonatal Edition*, 93, F115–F120.

23 Viswanathan, M. (1993). Measurement of individual differences in preference for numerical information. *Journal of Applied Psychology*, 78, 741–752.

24 Hallowell, N., Statham, H., Murton, F., Green, J., and Richards, M. (1997). "Talking about chance": The presentation of risk information during genetic counseling for breast and ovarian cancer. *Journal of Genetic Counseling*, 6, 269–286.

25 Parrott, R., Silk, K., and Condit, C. (2003). Diversity in lay perceptions of the sources of human traits: Genes, environments, and personal behaviors. *Social Science and Medicine*, 56, 1099–1109.

26 Adelsward, V., and Sachs, L. (1996). The meaning of 6.8: Numeracy and normality in health information talks. *Social Science and Medicine*, 8, 1179–1187.

27 Covello, V. T., and Peters, R. G. (2002). Women's perceptions of the risks of age-related diseases, including breast cancer: Reports from a three-year research study. *Health Communication*, 14, 377–395.

28 Wilson, S., Johnston, A., Robson, J., Poulter, N., Collier, D., Feder, G., and Caulfield, M. J. (2003). Comparison of methods to identify individuals at increased risk of coronary disease from the general population. *British Medical Journal*, 326, 1436–1441.

29 Lobb, E. A., Butow, P. N., Kenny, D. T., and Tattersall, M. H. N. (1999). Communicating prognosis in early breast cancer: Do women understand the language used? *Medical Journal of Australia*, 171, 290–294.

30 Lussier, G. (1996). Sex and mathematical background as predictors of anxiety and self-efficacy in mathematics. *Psychological Reports*, 79, 827–833.

31 Betz, N. E. (1978). Prevalence, distribution, and correlates of math anxiety in college students. *Journal of Counseling Psychology*, 25(5), 441–448.

32 Cooper, S. E., and Robinson, D. A. (1991). The relationship of mathematics self-efficacy beliefs to mathematics anxiety and performance. *Measurement and Evaluation in Counseling and Development*, 24, 4–11.

33 Newman, K. (2005). The case for the narrative brain. *ACM International Conference Proceeding Series*, 23, 145–149.

34 Mathieson, C. M. and Stam, H. J. (1995). Renegotiating identity: Cancer narratives. *Sociology of Health and Illness*, 17, 283–306.

35 Ochs, E. and Capps, L. (1996). Narrating the self. *Annual Review of Anthropology*, 25, 19–43.

36 American Cancer Society, Support for survivors and patients (2008). Retrieved from http:www.cancer.org/docroot/SHR/SHR_0.asp, on 9/11/2008.

37 Salander, P. (2002). Bad news from the patient's perspective: An analysis of the written narratives of newly diagnosed cancer patients. *Social Science and Medicine*, 55, 721–732.

38 Gotcher, J. M. (1995). Well-adjusted and maladjusted cancer patients: An examination of communication variables. *Health Communication*, 7, 21–33.

39 Bylund, C. L. (2005). Mothers' involvement in decision making during the birthing process: A quantitative analysis of women's online birth stories. *Health Communication*, 18, 23–39.

40 Sepucha, K. R., Belkora, J. K., Mutchnick, S., and Esserman, L. J. (2002). Consultation planning to help breast cancer patients prepare for medical consultations: Effect on communication and satisfaction for patients and physicians. *Journal of Clinical Oncology*, 20, 2695–2700.

41 Parrott, R., Volkman, J., Ghetian, C., Weiner, C., Weiner, J., Raup-Krieger, J., and Parrott, J. (2008). Memorable messages about genes and health: Implications for direct-to-consumer marketing of genetics tests and therapies. *Health Marketing Quarterly*, 25(1), 1–25.

42 Singer, J. A. (2004). Narrative identity and meaning making across the adult lifespan: An introduction. *Journal of Personality*, 72, 437–460.

43 Curlin, F. A., Roach, C. J., Gorawara-Bhat, R., Lantos, J. D., and Chin, M. H. (2005). When patients choose faith over medicine: Physician perspectives on religiously related conflict in the medical encounter. *Archives of Internal Medicine*, 165, 88–91.

44 Centers for Disease Control and Prevention (1993, July 16). Lead poisoning associated with use of traditional ethnic remedies – California, 1991–1992. *Morbidity and Mortality Weekly Report*, 42, 521–524.

45 Ouellette, J. A., and Wood, W. (1998). Habit and intention in everyday life: The multiple processes by which past behavior predicts future behavior. *Psychological Bulletin*, 124, 54–74.

46 Schreiber, L. (2005). The importance of precision in language: Communication research and (so-called) alternative medicine. *Health Communication*, 17, 173–190.

47 Committee on the Use of Complementary and Alternative Medicine (2005). *Complementary and Alternative Medicine in the United States*. Washington, DC: The National Academies Press.

48 Conner, M., Kirk, S. F., Cade, J. E., and Barrett, J. H. (2001). Why do women use dietary supplements? The use of the theory of planned behaviour to explore beliefs about their use. *Social Science and Medicine,* 52, 621–633.

49 Clegg, D. O., Reda, D. J., Harris, C. L., Klein, M. A., O'Dell, J. R., Hooper, M. M., Bradley, J. D., Bingham III, C. O., Weisman, M. H., Jackson, C. G., Lane, N. E., Cush, J. J., Moreland, J. W., Schumacher, R., Oddis, C. V., Wolfe, F., Molitor, J. A., Yocum, D. E., Scnitzer, T. J., Furst, D. E., Sawitzke, A. D., Shi, H., Brandt, K. D., Moskowitz, R. W., and Williams, H. J. (2006). Glucosamine, chondroitin sulfate, and the two in combination for painful knee osteoarthritis. *New England Journal of Medicine,* 354, 795–808.

50 Howell, L., Kochhar, K., Saywell, R., Zollinger, T., Koehler, J., Mandzuk, C., Sutton, B., Sevilla-Martir, J., and Allen, D. (2006). Use of herbal remedies by Hispanic patients: Do they inform their physician? *Journal of the American Board of Family Physicians,* 19, 566–578.

51 American Occupational Therapy Association, Inc., Living with spinal cord injury (SCI). Retrieved from www.aota.org/Consumers/Tips/Conditions/SCI/35189.aspx, on 9/11/2008.

52 Parrott, R., Stuart, T., and Cairns, A. B. (2000). Reducing uncertainty through communication during adjustment to disability: Living with spinal cord injury. In D. O. Braithwaite and T. L. Thompson (eds), *Handbook of Communication and People with Disabilities: Research and application* (pp. 339–352). Mahwah, NJ: Lawrence Erlbaum.

53 Kaplowitz, S. A., Campo, S., and Chiu, W. T. (2002). Cancer patients' desires for communication of prognosis information. *Health Communication,* 14, 221–241.

54 Ajaj, A., Singh, M. P., and Abdulla, A. J. J. (2001). Should elderly patients be told they have cancer? Questionnaire survey of older people. *British Medical Journal,* 323, 1160.

55 Houldin, A. D. (2007). A qualitative study of caregivers' experiences with newly diagnosed advanced colorectal cancer. *Oncology Nursing Forum,* 34, 323–330.

56 Gray, R. E., Fitch, M., Phillips, C., Labrecque, M., and Fergus, K. (2000). To tell or not to tell: Patterns of disclosure among men with prostate cancer. *Psycho-Oncology,* 9, 273–282.

57 Arrington, M. I. (2005). "She's right behind me all the way": An analysis of prostate cancer narratives and changes in family relationships. *Journal of Family Communication,* 5, 141–162.

58 Kendall, S., (2006). Being asked not to tell: Nurses' experiences of caring for patients not told their diagnosis. *Journal of Clinical Nursing,* 15, 1149–1157.

59 Keeley, M. P., and Yingling, J. M. (2007). *Final Conversations: Helping the living and the dying talk to each other.* Acton, MA: Van Wyk and Burnham.

60 Gaskin, D. J., Kong, J., Meropol, N. J., Yabroff, K. R., Weaver, C., and Schulman, K. A. (1998). Treatment choices by serious ill patients. *Medical Decision Making,* 18, 84–94.

61 Parle, M., Maguire, P., and Heaven, C. (1997). The development of a training model to improve health professionals' skills, self-efficacy and outcome expectancies when communicating with cancer patients. *Social Science and Medicine,* 44, 231–240.

3 What Are My "Risk" Factors?

62 Wysocki, T., Green, L., and Huxtable, K. (1989). Blood glucose monitoring by diabetic adolescents: Compliance and metabolic control. *Health Psychology,* 8, 267–284.

63 Gray, J. A. (1982). *The Neuropsychology of Anxiety: An enquiry into the functions of the septo-hippocampal system.* New York: Oxford University Press.

64 Carver, C. S. and White, T. L. (1994). Behavioral inhibition, behavioral activation, and affective responses to impending reward and punishment: The BIS/BAS scales. *Journal of Personality and Social Psychology,* 67, 319–333.

65 Luciana, M., Collins, P. F., and Depue, R. A. (1992). Opposing roles for dopamine and serotonin in the modulation of human spatial working memory functions. *Cerebral Cortex,* 8, 218–226.

66 Corrigall, W. A., Coen, K. M., and Adamson, K. L. (1994). Self-administered nicotine activates the mesolimbic dopamine system through the ventral tegmental area. *Brain Research,* 653, 278–284.

67 Rodway, P., Dienses, Z., and Schepman, A. (2000). The effects of cigarette smoking on negative priming. *Experimental and Clinical Psychopharmacology,* 8, 104–111.

68 Jorm, A. F., Christensen, H., Henderson, A. S., Jacomb, P. A., Korten, A. E., and Rodgers, B. (1998). Using the BIS/BAS scales to measure behavioural inhibition and behavioural activation: Factor structure, validity and norms in a large community sample. *Personality and Individual Differences,* 26, 49–58.

69 Cooper, M. L., Agocha, V. B., and Sheldon, M. S. (2000). A motivational perspective on risky behaviors: The role of personality and affect regulatory processes. *Journal of Personality,* 68, 1059–1088.

70   McFarland, B. R., Shankman, S. A., Tenke, C. E., Bruder, G. E., and Klein, D. N. (2006). Behavioral activation system deficits predict the six-month course of depression. *Journal of Affective Disorders*, 91, 229–234.

71   Gray 1982; Carver and White 1994: see 63 and 64 above.

72   Spoont, M. R. (1992). Modulatory role of serotonin in neural information processing: Implications for human psychopathology. *Psychological Bulletin*, 11, 330–350.

73   Luciana et al. 1998. See 65 above.

74   Henriksen, L., and Jackson, C. (1998). Anti-smoking socialization: Relationship to parent and child smoking status. *Health Communication*, 10, 87–101.

75   Kambouropoulos, N., and Staiger, P. K. (2004). Reactivity to alcohol-related cues: Relationship among cue type, motivational processes, and personality. *Psychology of Addictive Behaviors*, 18, 275–283.

76   Lobb et al. (1999). See 29 above.

77   Clayton, R. R., Segress, M. J. H., and Caudill, C. A. (2007). Sensation-seeking: A commentary. *Addiction*, 102, 92–94.

78   Holtgrave, D. R., Tinsley, B. J., and Kay, L. S. (1995). Encouraging risk reduction: A decision-making approach to message design. In E. Maibach and R. Parrott (eds.), *Designing Health Messages: Approaches from communication theory and public health practice* (pp. 24–40). Thousand Oaks, CA: Sage.

79   Netter, P., Hennig, J., and Roed, I. S. (1996). Serotonin and dopamine as mediators of sensation seeking behavior. *Biological Psychology/Pharmacopsychology*, 34, 155–165.

80   Zuckerman, M. (1990). The psychophysiology of sensation seeking. *Journal of Personality*, 58, 313–345.

81   Donohew, L., Zimmerman, R., Cupp, P. S., Novak, S., Colon, S., and Abell, R. (2000). Sensation seeking, impulsive decision-making, and risky sex: Implications for risk-taking and design of interventions. *Personality and Individual Differences*, 28, 1079–1091.

82   Kassinove, J. I. (1998). Development of the gambling attitude scales: Preliminary findings. *Journal of Clinical Psychology*, 54, 763–771.

83   Laucht, M., Becker, K., and Schmidt, M. H. (2006). Visual exploratory behaviour in infancy and novelty seeking in adolescence: Two developmentally specific phenotypes of DRD4? *Journal of Child Psychology and Psychiatry*, 47, 1143–1151.

84   Niederdeppe, J., Davis, K. C., Farrelly, M. C., and Yarsevich, J. (2007). Stylistic features, need for sensation, and confirmed recall of national smoking prevention advertisements. *Journal of Communication*, 57, 272–292.

85   Sirois, F. M. (2006). "I'll look after my health later": A replication and extension of the procrastination-health model with community-dwelling adults. *Personality and Individual Differences*, 43, 15–26.

86   Miller, S. M., Siejak, K. K., Schroeder, C. M., Lerman, C., Hernandez, E., and Helm, C. W. (1997). Enhancing adherence following abnormal Pap smears among low-income minority women: A preventive telephone counseling strategy. *Journal of the National Cancer Institute*, 89, 703–708.

87   Passanisi, N., Prout, M., and Holm, L. J. (2001). The New England division "Tell a Friend" program implementation evaluation. *Cancer Practice*, 9 (Suppl. 1), S64–S71.

88   Davis, T. C., Wolf, M. S., Bass, P. F., Middlebrooks, M., Kennen, E., Baker, D. W., Bennette, C. L., Durazo-Arvizu, R., Bocchini, A., Savory, S., and Parker, R. M. (2006). Low literacy impairs comprehension of prescription drug warning labels. *Journal of General Internal Medicine*, 21, 847–851.

89   Scheitel, S. M., Boland, B. J., Wollan, P. C., and Silverstein, M. D. (1996). Patient–physician agreement about medical diagnoses and cardiovascular risk factors in the ambulatory general medical examination. *Mayo Clinical Proceedings*, 71, 1131–1137.

90   Parrott, R., Monahan, J., Ainsworth, S., and Steiner, C. (1998). Communicating to farmers about skin cancer: A behavioral adaptation model. *Human Communication Research*, 24, 386–409.

91   Schneider, A., and McCumber, D. (2005). *An Air that Kills: How the asbestos poisoning of Libby, Montana, uncovered a national scandal.* New York: Penguin Books.

92   Chatters, L. M., Levin, J. S., and Taylor, R. J. (1992). Antecedents and dimensions of religious involvement among older black adults. *Journal of Gerontology*, 47 (suppl.), 269–278.

93   Kerr, A., Cunningham-Burley, S., and Amos, A. (1998). Drawing the line: An analysis of lay discussions about the new genetics. *Public Understanding of Science*, 7, 113–133.

94   Harris, T., Parrott, R., and Dorgan, K. (2004). Talking about human genetics within religious frameworks. *Health Communication*, 16(1), 105–116.

95   Parrott, R., Silk, K., Krieger, J. R., Harris, T., and Condit, C. (2004). Behavioral health outcomes associated with religious faith and media exposure about human genetics. *Health Communication*, 16(1), 29–46.

96   Ellison, C. G., and Goodson, P. (1997). Conservative Protestantism and attitudes toward family planning in a sample of seminarians. *Journal for the Scientific Study of Religion*, 36, 512–529.

97   Franken, I. H. A., and Muris, P. (2006). BIS/BAS personality characteristics and college students' substance use. *Personality and Individual Differences*, 40, 1497–1503.

98   Soweid, R. A. A., Khawaja, M., and Salem, M. T. (2004). Religious identity and smoking behavior among adolescents: Evidence from entering

students at the American University of Beirut. *Health Communication*, 16, 47–62.

99 Sloan, R. P., Bagiella, E., and Powell, T. (1999). Religion, spirituality, and medicine. *The Lancet*, 353, 664–667.

100 Peters, T. (1997). *Playing God? Genetic determinism and human freedom.* New York: Routledge.

101 Valenti, J. M. (2002). Communication challenges for science and religion. *Public Understanding of Science*, 11, 57–63.

4 Why Don't We Get "Care"?

102 Ross, S., Grant, A., Counsell, C., Gillespie, W., Russell, I., and Prescott, R. (1999). Barriers to participation in randomized controlled trials: Literature summary and annotated bibliography. *Journal of Clinical Epidemiology*, 52, 1143–1156.

103 Gostin, L. O. (1995). Informed consent, cultural sensitivity, and respect for persons. *Journal of the American Medical Association*, 274, 844–845.

104 Sugarman, J., and Powers, M. (1991). How the doctor got gagged. The disintegrating right of privacy in the physician–patient relationship. *Journal of the American Medical Association*, 266, 3323–3327.

105 Milone, S. D., and Milone, S. L. (2006). Evidence-based periodic health examination of adults: Memory aid for primary care physicians. *Canadian Family Physician*, 10, 40–47.

106 Davidhizar, R., and Giger, J. N. (1994). A review of the literature on care of clients in pain who are culturally diverse. *International Nursing Review*, 51, 47–55.

107 Speice, J., Harkness, J., Laneri, H., Frankel, R., Roter, D., Kornblith, A. B., Ahles, T., Winer, E., Fleishman, S., Luber, P., Zevon, M., McQuellon, R., Trief, P., Finkel, J., Spira, J., Greenberg, D., Towland, J., and Holland, J. C. (2000). Involving family members in cancer care: Focus group considerations of patients and oncological providers. *Psycho-Oncology*, 9, 101–112.

108 Leydon, G. M., Bynoe-Sutherland, J., and Coleman, M. P. (2003). The journey towards a cancer diagnosis: The experiences of people with cancer, their family and carers. *European Journal of Cancer Care*, 12, 317–326.

109 Majerovitz, S. D., Greene, M. G., Adelman, R. D., Brody, G. M., Leber, K., and Healy, S. W. (1997). Older patients' understanding of medical information in the emergency department. *Health Communication*, 9, 237–251.

110 Morisky, D. E., DeMuth, N. M., Field-Fass, M., Green, L. W., and Levine, D. M. (1985). Evaluation of family health education to build social support for long-term control of high blood pressure. *Health Education Quarterly*, 12, 35–50.

111 Korhonen, T., Uutela, A., Korhonen, H. J., and Puska, P. (1998). Impact of mass media and interpersonal health communication on smoking cessation attempts: A study in North Karelia, 1989–1996. *Journal of Health Communication*, 3, 105–118.

112 Committee on the Consequences of Uninsurance (2002). *Health Insurance Is a Family Matter*. Washington, DC: The National Academies Press.

113 Stiggelbout, A. M., Jansen, S. J. T., Otten, W., Baas-Thijssen, M. C. M., van Slooten, H., and van de Velde, C. J. J. (2007). How important is the opinion of significant others to cancer patients' adjuvant chemotherapy decision-making? *Supportive Care in Cancer*, 15, 319–325.

114 Koerner, A. F., and Cvancara, K. E. (2002). The influence of conformity orientation on communication patterns in family conversations. *Journal of Family Communication*, 2, 133–152.

115 Lewin, S. A., Babigumira, S. M., Bosch-Capblanch, X., van Wyk, A. G., Glenton, C., Scheel, I., Zwarenstein, M., and Daniels, K. (2006, November). Lay health workers in primary and community health care: A systematic review of trials. Retrieved from (www.who.int/rpc/meetings/LHW_review.pdf), on 9/26/2008.

116 Baldwin, J. R., Faulkner, S., Hecht, M., Lindsley, S. L. (2005). *Redefining Culture: Perspectives across the disciplines*. Mahwah, NJ: Lawrence Erlbaum Associates.

117 Airhihenbuwa, C. O., Makinwa, B., and Obregon, R. (2000). Toward a new communications framework for HIV/AIDS. *Journal of Health Communication*, 5, 101–111.

118 Brown, P., Levinson, S. C., and Gumperz, J. L. (1987). *Politeness: Some universals in language usage*. New York: Cambridge University Press.

119 Horwitz, S. M., Leaf, P. J., and Leventhal, J. M. (1998). Identification of psychosocial problems in pediatric primary care. *Archives of Pediatric Adolescent Medicine*, 152, 367–371.

120 Majerovitz et al. 1997. See 109 above.

121 Chapple, A., and Ziebland, S. (2002). Prostate cancer: Embodied experience and perceptions of masculinity. *Sociology of Health and Illness*, 24, 820–841.

122 Weiner, J. L., Silk, K. J., and Parrott, R. L. (2005). Family communication and genetic health: A research note. *Journal of Family Communication*, 5, 313–324.

123 Johnson, J. L., Bottorff, J. L., and Browne, A. J. (2004). Othering and being othered in the context of health care services. *Health Communication*, 16, 253–271.

124 Weinstein, N. D. (1987). Unrealistic optimism about susceptibility to health problems: Conclusions from a community-wide sample. *Journal of Behavioral Medicine*, 10, 481–500.

125 Horswill, M. S., and Mckenna, F. P. (1999). The effect of perceived control on risk taking. *Journal of Applied Social Psychology*, 29, 377–391.

126 Arnett, J. J. (2000). Optimistic bias in adolescent and adult smokers and nonsmokers. *Addictive Behaviors*, 25, 625–632.

127 Weinstein, N. D. (1982). Unrealistic optimism about susceptibility to health problems. *Journal of Behavioral Medicine*, 5, 441–460.

128 Renn, O., Burns, W. J., Kasperson, J. X., Kasperson, R. E., and Slovic, P. (1992). The social amplification of risk: Theoretical foundations and empirical applications. *Journal of Social Issues*, 48, 137–160.

5 Is the "Public Good" Good for Me?

129 Glasgow, Fisher, et al.; Glasgow, Wagner, et al. See 9 above.

130 Zuckerman, B., Stevens, G. D., Inkelas, M., and Halfon, N. (2004). Prevalence and correlates of high-quality basic pediatric preventive care. *Pediatrics*, 114, 1522–1529.

131 Covello and Peters (2002). See 27 above.

132 LeGales, C., Bougerol, C., Fainzang, S., Seror, V., Galacteros, F., Bardakdjian, J., and Assaba, C. (1993). Economic assessment of new-born screening for sickle cell disease in France. *Abstracts of the International Society of Technological Assessments in Health Care Meeting*, 9, 163.

133 Patch, C. (2006). Newborn screening policy in the United Kingdom and the United States: Two different communities of practice. *American Journal of Maternal and Child Nursing*, 31, 164–168. March of Dimes, Professionals and Researchers: Clinical issues and considerations. Newborn screening: Introduction and history. Retrieved from www.marchofdimes.com/printableArticles/24279_9606.asp, 9/18/2008.

134 Welcome to the UK Newborn Screening Programme Centre. Retrieved from www.newbornscreening-bloodspot.org.uk, on 7/9/2008.

135 Centers for Disease Control and Protection, Nationally notifiable infectious diseases. Retrieved from www.cdc.gov/ncphi/disss/nndss/phs/infdis.htm, on 9/25/2008.

136 Parrott, R., Silk, K., Dillow, M., Krieger, J., Harris, T., and Condit, T. (2005). The development and validation of tools to assess perceptions of genetic discrimination and genetic racism. *Journal of the National Medical Association*, 97, 980–991.

137 Salmon, D. A., Haber, M., Gangaros, E. J., Phillips, L., Smith, N. J., and Chen, R. T. (1999). Health consequences of religious and philosophical

exemptions from immunization laws. *Journal of the American Medical Association*, 282, 47–53.

138 McIlroy, C. (2004). Issue brief: Bioterrorism and state public health laws – new challenges. Retrieved from www.nga.org/cda/files/0405BIOTERRORISMLAWS.pdf, on 9/23/2008.

139 Apollonio, D. E., and Bero, L. A. (2007). Protecting the public from environmental hazards: The creation of industry front groups: The tobacco industry and "get government off our back." *American Journal of Public Health*, 97, 419–427.

140 Sinclair, U. (1906). *The Jungle*. New York: Doubleday.

141 US Food and Drug Administration, Center for Drug Evaluation and Research, Investigational new drug (IND) application process. Retrieved from www.fda.gov/cder/Regulatory/applications/ind_page_1.htm, on 9/21/2008.

142 Drake, A. W., Finkelstein, S. N., and Sapolsky, H. M. (1982). *The American Blood Supply: Issues and policies of blood donation. Health and public policy*. Cambridge, MA: MIT Press.

143 Lyme disease and babesiosis blood donations: Blood donation centers. Retrieved from www.lymeinfo.net/bloodtransfusions.html, on 7/11/2008.

144 Engholm, G., Palmgren, F., and Lynge, E. (1996). Lung cancer, smoking, and environment: A cohort study of the Danish population. *British Medical Journal*, 312, 1259–1263.

145 US Environmental Protection Agency, Asthma and indoor environments: About asthma. Retrieved from www.epa.gov/ashthma/about.html, on 10/28/2006.

146 US Environmental Protection Agency, The Safe Drinking Water Act and lead in drinking water. Retrieved from www.epa.gov/safewater/lcmr/lead_nsfstandard.html, on 7/11/2008.

147 European Public Health Alliance, Update 67: Water: Preventing a crisis. Retrieved from www.epha.org/a/276 on 7/16/2008.

148 Hammond, D., Fong, G. T., Borland, R., Cummings, K. M., McNeil, A., and Driezen, P. (2007). Text and graphic warnings on cigarette packages: Findings from the international tobacco control four country study. *American Journal of Preventive Medicine*, 32, 202–209.

149 De Turck, M. (2002). Persuasive effects of product warning labels. In J. P. Dillard and M. Pfau (eds), *The Persuasion Handbook: Developments in theory and practice* (pp. 345–370). Thousand Oaks, CA: Sage.

150 Cantrill, J. G. (1993). Communication and our environment: Categorizing research in environmental advocacy. *Journal of Applied Communication Research*, 21(1), 66–95. Cantrill, J. G. (1998). The environmental self and a sense of place: Communication foundations for regional ecosystem management. *Journal of Applied Communication Research*, 26, 301–318.

151 Miller, K., and Zook, E. G. (1997). Care partners for persons with AIDS: Implications for health communication. *Journal of Applied Communication Research*, 25, 57–74.

152 Juniata Clean Water Partnership. Retrieved from www.jcwp.org/, on 9/23/2008.

153 Thompson, T. and Parrott, R. (2002). Interpersonal communication and health care. In M. Knapp and J. Daly (eds), *Handbook of Interpersonal Communication*, 3rd edn (pp. 680–725). Thousand Oaks, CA: Sage.

154 Pratt, C. B., Ha, L., and Pratt, C. A. (2002). Setting the public health agenda on major diseases in sub-Saharan Africa: African popular magazines and medical journals, 1981–1997. *Journal of Communication*, 52, 889–904.

155 Sandman, P. M., Weinstein, N. D., and Klotz, M. L. (1987). Public response to the risk from geological radon. *Journal of Communication*, 37(3), 93–108.

156 Callahan, D., and Jennings, B. (2002). Ethics and public health: Forging a strong relationship. *American Journal of Public Health*, 92, 169–176.

6 Who Profits from My Health?

157 UK pharma: Key player – AstraZeneca. Retrieved from www.eiu.com/index.asp?layout=ib3Article&article_id=2003904185&pubtypeid=1152462500&rf=0 on 12/ 21/2008.

158 Dens, N., Eagle, L. C., and De Pelsmacker, P. (2008). Attitudes and self-reported behavior of patients, doctors, and pharmacists in New Zealand and Belgium toward direct-to-consumer advertising of medication. *Health Communication*, 23, 45–61.

159 Davis, J. J., Cross, E., and Crowley, J. (2007). Pharmaceutical websites and the communication of risk information. *Journal of Health Communication*, 12, 29–39.

160 Kravitz, R. L., Epstein, R. J., Feldman, M. D., Franz, C. E., Azari, R., Wilkes, M. S., Hinton, L., and Franks, P. (2005). Influence of patients' requests for direct-to-consumer advertised antidepressants: A randomized controlled trial. *Journal of the American Medical Association*, 293, 1995–2002.

161 Hollon, M. F. (1999). Direct-to-consumer marketing of prescription drugs: A current perspective for neurologists and psychiatrists. *CNS Drugs*, 18, 69–77.

162 Abel, G. A., Penson, R. T., Joffe, S., Schapira, L., Chabner, B. A., and Lynch, T. J. (2007). Direct-to-consumer advertising in oncology. *The Oncologist*, 11, 217–226.

163 Lyon, A. (2007). "Putting patients first": Systematically distorted communication and Merck's marketing of Vioxx. *Journal of Applied Communication Research*, 35, 376–398.

164 Freimuth, V. S., Hammond, S. L., and Stein, J. A. (1988). Health advertising: Prevention for profit. *American Journal of Public Health*, 78, 557–561.

165 Smith, S. C., Taylor, J. G., and Stephen, A. M. (1999). Use of food labels and beliefs about diet–disease relationships among university students. *Public Health Nutrition*, 3, 175–182.

166 Food Safety Authority of Ireland (2007). The labelling of food in Ireland. Retrieved from www.fsai.ie/publications/reports/labelling2007.pdf, on 7/16/2008.

167 Better labeling urged after teen's sports cream overdoes: BenGay maker says it is safe when used as directed (2007, June 12). Retrieved from http://seattlepi.nwsource.com/printer2/index.asp?ploc=tandrefer=http://seattlepi.nwsource.com/health/319572_cream13.html, on 9/24/2008.

168 Wang, Z., and Gantz, W. (2007). Health content in local television news. *Health Communication*, 21, 213–221.

169 Slattery, K., Doremus, M., and Marcus, L. (2001). Shifts in public affairs reporting on the network evening news: A move toward the sensational. *Journal of Broadcasting and Electronic Media*, 45, 290–302.

170 Bell, A. (1991). *The Language of News Media*. Cambridge, MA: Basil Blackwell.

171 Moyer, A., Greener, S., Beauvais, J., and Salovey, P. (1995). Accuracy of health research reported in the popular press: Breast cancer mammography. *Health Communication*, 7, 147–161.

172 Pellechia, M. G. (1997). Trends in science coverage: A content analysis of three US newspapers. *Public Understanding of Science*, 6, 49–68.

173 Conrad, P. (1999). Uses of expertise: Sources, quotes, and voice in the reporting of genetics in the news. *Public Understanding of Science*, 8, 285–302.

174 Hoskins, K. F., Stopfer, J. E., Calzone, K. A., Merajver, S. D., Rebbeck, T. R., Garber, J. E., and Weber, B. L. (1995). Assessment and counseling for women with a family history of breast cancer: A guide for clinicians. *Journal of the American Medical Association*, 273, 577–585.

175 Sundar, S. S. (2000). Conceptualizing sources in online news. *Journal of Communication*, 51, 52–72.

176 Bahk, C. M. (2001). Drench effects of media portrayal of fatal virus disease on health locus of control beliefs. *Health Communication*, 13, 187–204.

177 Parrott et al. 2008., See 41 above.

178   Centers for Disease Control and Prevention, Health Marketing – Healthstyles Survey. Retrieved from www.cdc.gov/HealthMarketing/ entertainment_education/healthstyles_survey.htm, on 9/24/2008.

179   Outley, C. W. and Taddese, A. (2006). A content analysis of health and physical activity messages marketed to African American children during after-school television programming. *Archives of Pediatrics and Adolescent Medicine*, 160, 432–435.

180   Galician, M. L. (2004). Product placement in the mass media: Unholy marketing marriages or realistic story-telling portrayals, unethical advertising messages or useful communication practices? *Journal of Promotion Management*, 10(1), 1–8.

181   Brandcameo – films. Retrieved from www.brandchannel.com/ brandcameo_films.asp, on 9/24/2008.

182   Interbrand: Creating and managing brand value. Retrieved from www.interbrand.com, on 9/21/2008.

183   Siegel, P. (2004). Product placement and the law. *Journal of Promotion Management*, 10(1), 89–100.

184   Hazan, A. R., and Glantz, S. A. (1995). Current trends in tobacco use on prime-time fictional television. *American Journal of Public Health*, 85, 116–117.

185   McGee, R., and Ketchel, J. (2006). Tobacco imagery on New Zealand television: 2002–2004. *Tobacco Control*, 15, 412–414.

186   Mathios, A., Averty, R., Biscogni, C., and Shanahan, J. (1998). Alcohol portrayal on prime-time television: Manifest and latent messages. *Journal of Studies on Alcohol*, 59, 305–310.

187   Signorielli, N., and Lears, M. (1992). Television and children's conceptions of nutrition: Unhealthy messages. *Health Communication*, 4, 245–257.

188   Greenberg, B. S., Eastin, M., Hofschire, L., Lachlan, K., and Brownell, K. D. (2003). Portrayals of overweight and obese individuals on commercial television. *American Journal of Public Health*, 93, 1342–1348.

189   Galician 2004. See 180 above.

190   The Communication Initiative Network: Hollywood, Health & Society – United States. Retrieved from www.comminit.com/en/node/123490, on 9/21/2008.

191   Wilson, K. E., and Beck, V. H. (2002). Entertainment outreach for women's health at CDC. *Journal of Women's Health and Gender-Based Medicine*, 11, 575–578.

192   Boden, W. E., and Diamond, G. A. (2008). DTCA for PTCA – Crossing the line in consumer health education? *New England Journal of Medicine*, 358, 2197–2200.

193 Stevenson, H. W., Lee, S. Y., and Stigler, J. W. (1986). Mathematics achievement of Chinese, Japanese, and American children. *Science*, 231, 693–699.

194 Salili, F. (1996). Accepting personal responsibility for learning. In D. A. Watkins and J. B. Biggs (eds), *The Chinese Learner: Cultural, psychological and contextual influences* (pp. 85–105). Hong Kong and Melbourne: Comparative Education Resource Center (CERC) and Australian Council for Educational Research (ACER).

195 Williams, M. V., Parker, R. M., Baker, D. W., Parikh, N. S., Pitkin, K., Coates, W. C., and Nurss, J. R. (1995). Inadequate functional health literacy among patients at two public hospitals. *Journal of the American Medical Association*, 274, 1677–1682.

196 Reys, B. J., Dingman, S., Nevels, N., and Teuscher, D. (2007). High school mathematics: State-level curriculum standards and graduation requirements. Center for the Study of Mathematics Curriculum. Retrieved from www.mathcurriculumcenter.org/PDFS/HSreport.pdf, on 9/24/2008.

197 Cooper, C. P., and Yukimura, D. (2002). Science writers' reactions to a medical "breakthrough" story. *Social Science and Medicine*, 54, 1887–1896.

7 What's Politics Got To Do with It?

198 Levin, A. (2001). The Cochrane collection. *Annals of Internal Medicine*, 135, 309–312.

199 Markman, M., Petersen, J., and Montgomery, R. (2006). Influence of tumor type, disease status, and patient age on self-reported interest regarding participation in cancer clinical trials. *Cancer*, 107, 849–853.

200 FDA drug approval process. Retrieved from www.chemcases.com/cisplat/cisplat15.htm, retrieved on 9/24/2008.

201 Raup-Krieger, J., Parrott, R., and Nussbaum, J. (under review). An empirical test of metaphors as a strategy for creating culturally appropriate messages. *Journal of Health Communication*.

202 Moseley, J. B., O'Malley, K., Petersen, N. J., Menke, T. J., Brody, B. A., Kuykendall, D. H., Hollingsworth, J. C., Ashton, C. M., and Wray, N. P. (2002). A controlled trial of arthroscopic surgery for osteoarthritis of the knee. *New England Journal of Medicine*, 347, 81–88.

203 Bhattaram, V. A., Booth, B. P., Ramchandani, R. P., Beasley, B. N., Wang, Y., Tandon, V., Duan, J. Z., Baweja, R. K., Marroum, P. J., Uppoor, R. S., Rahman, N. A., Sahajwall, C. G., Powell, J. R., Mehta, M. U., and Gobburu, J. V. S. (2005). Impact of pharmacometrics on drug

approval and labeling decisions: A survey of 42 new drug applications. *AAPS Journal*, 7, E503–E5112.

204 Gardin, J. M., Schumacher, D., Constantine, G., Davis, K. D., Leung, C., and Reid, C. L. (2000). Valvular abnormalities and cardiovascular status following exposure to dexfenfluramine or phentermine/fenfluramine. *Journal of the American Medical Association*, 283, 1703–1709.

205 Sachdev, M., Miller, W. C., Ryan, T., and Jollis, J. G. (2002). Effect of fenfluamine-derivative diet pills on cardiac valves: A meta-analysis of observational studies. *American Heart Journal*, 144, 1065–1073.

206 Chen, D. A., Backous, D. D., Arriaga, M. A., Garvin, R., Kobyle, D., Littman, T., Walgren, S., and Lura, D. (2004). Phase 1 clinical trial results of the envoy system: A totally implantable middle ear device for sensorineural hearing loss. *Otolaryngology – Head and Neck Surgery*, 131, 904–916.

207 Rodriuez, E., DePuelles, P. E., and Jovell, A. J. (1999). The Spanish health care system: Lessons for newly industrialized countries. *Health Policy and Planning*, 14, 164–173.

208 Embassy of France (2007, January 10). The French healthcare system. Retrieved from www.info-france-usa.org.atoz/health.asp, on 1/10/2007.

209 Drexler, M. (2003). *Health Disparities and the Body Politic: A series of international symposia*. Boston, MA: Harvard School of Public Health. Retrieved from www.hsph.harvard.edu/disparities/book/index.html, on 9/25/2008.

210 The color of research. Retrieved from www.tufts.edu/home/feature/ ?p=tuskegee, on 7/25/2008.

211 Dober, G. (2008). Cheaper than chimpanzees: Expanding the use of prisoners in medical experiments. *Prison Legal News*. Retrieved from www.prisonlegalnews.org/displayArticle.aspx?articleid=19630&AspxAuto DetectCookieSupport=1, on 9/25/2008.

212 Institute of Medicine (2006). *Ethical Considerations for Research Involving Prisoners*. Washington DC: National Academies Press.

213 Eslocker, A. R., and Hill, A. (2006, July 7). Artificial blood experiment: Is your city participating? Retrieved from http://abcnews.go.com/WNT/ story?id=2166058&page=1&WNT=true, on 9/25/2008.

214 Natanson, C., Kern, S. J., Lurie, P., Banks, S. M., and Wolfe, S. M. (2008). Cell-free hemoglobin-based blood substitutes and risk of myocardial infarction and death. *Journal of the American Medical Association*, 299, 2304–2312.

215 *Medical News Today* (2008, July 10). Largest international cardiac surgery study will compare open-heart surgery with or without heart-lung machine. Retrieved from www.medicalnewstoday.com/ printerfriendlynews.php?newsid=114476, on 7/24/2008.

216 National Conference of State Legislatures (2007, November). Pharmacist conscience clauses: Laws and legislation. Retrieved from www.ncsl.org/programs/health/ConscienceClauses.htm, on 9/25/2008.

217 Hyde, M. J., and Rufo, K. (2000). The call of conscience, rhetorical interruptions, and the euthanasia controversy. *Journal of Applied Communication Research*, 28(1), 1–23.

218 Griffiths, J. (2008). Physician-assisted suicide in the Netherlands and Belgium. In D. Birnbacher and E. Dahl (eds), *Giving Death a Helping Hand: Physician-assisted suicide and public policy. An international perspective* (pp. 77–86). Dordrecht, The Netherlands: Springer.

219 Teri Schiavo. Retrieved from http://news.findlaw.com/legalnews/lit/ schiavo/, on 9/25/2008.

220 Paillaud, E., Ferrand, E., Lejonc, J., Henry, O., Bouillanne, O., and Montagne, O. (2007). Medical information and surrogate designation: Results of a prospective study in elderly hospitalized patients. *Age and Ageing*, 36, 274–279.

221 American Medical Association (2007). Position statement: Direct-to-consumer advertising. Retrieved from www.ama.com.au/web.nsf/doc/ WEEN-7AM7CH, on 7/26/2008.

222 Mishra, S. K. (2005, August 29). Telemedicine: Experience at a tertiary care hospital. Enterprise networking and computing in healthcare industry. Proceedings of the 7th International Workshop. Retrieved from http://ieeexplore.ieee.org/xpl/freeabs_all.jsp?arnumber=1500370, on 9/25/2008.

223 Harris, C. P. (1999). Lobbying and public affairs in the UK: The relationship to political marketing. PhD thesis, Manchester Metropolitan University. Retrieved from http://eprints.otago.ac.nz/378/, on 7/23/2008.

224 Lobbying Disclosure Act. Retrieved from www.senate.gov/legislative/ Lobbying/Lobby_Disclosure_Act/TOC.htm, on 9/25/2008.

225 Landers, S. H., and Sehgal, A. R. (2004). Health care lobbying in the United States. *American Journal of Medicine*, 116, 474–477.

226 Agnew, B. (1999). Peer review: NIH invites activists into the inner sanctum. *Science*, 283, 199–2001. Retrieved from www.sciencemag.org/ cgi/content/summary/283/5410/1999, on 9/25/2008.

227 Georgia Department of Community Health. Migrant health, homeless and special projects. Retrieved from http://dch.georgia.gov/00/channel_ title/0,2094,31446711_40951017,00.html, on 9/24/2008.ahgeor internet migrant.

228 UK NHS Centre for Involvement, www.nhscentreforinvolvement.nhs.uk, retrieved on 7/22/2008.

229 National Cancer Institute, Office of Advocacy Relations. Retrieved from http://ola.cancer.gov, on 9/24/2008.

230 National Cancer Institute, Office of Advocacy Relations (2008, September 8). Opportunities for public comment. Retrieved from http://ola.cancer.gov/activities/comment, on 9/24/2008. Cochrane Consumer Network. Retrieved from www.cochrane.org/consumers/homepage on 12/21/2008.

231 Walsh-Burke, K. (2001). Self-advocacy training for cancer survivors. *Cancer Practice*, 7, 297–301.

232 Brashers, D. E., Haas, S. M., Klingle, R. S., and Neidig, J. L. (2000). Collective AIDS activism and individuals' perceived self-advocacy in physician–patient communication. *Human Communication Research*, 26, 372–402.

233 Mosley, J. (2002). What leads human service nonprofits to be involved in advocacy? Testing a theoretical model that predicts advocacy involvement. Retrieved from http://arnova.omnibooksonline.com/2006/data/papers/PA061226.pdf, on 9/25/2008.

234 Teret, S. P., Alexander, G. R., and Bailey, L. A. (1990). The passage of Maryland's gun law: Data and advocacy for injury prevention. *Journal of Public Health Policy*, 11, 26–38.

235 Vernick, J. D. (1999). Lobbying and advocacy for the public's health: What are the limits on organizations? *American Journal of Public Health*, 89, 1425–1429.

236 Gordon, K. B. (2005). Patient education and advocacy groups: A means to better outcomes? *Archives of Dermatology*, 141, 80–81.

237 Wallack, L. and Dorfman, L. (2001). Media advocacy: A strategy for advancing policy and promoting health. *Health Education Quarterly*, 23, 293–317.

238 Muscular Dystrophy Association (2005, November 4). NIH names three new muscular dystrophy centers of excellence. Retrieved from www.mda.org/news/051104three_new_centers.html, on 9/24/2008.

8 An Agenda for the Twenty-first Century

239 Methylenetetrahydrofolate reductase polymorphism (MTHFR). Retrieved from http://pathology.mc.duke.edu/coag/MRHFR1flyer2.html, on 7/30/2008.

240 Fowler, B. (1998). Genetic defects of folate and cobalamin metabolism. *European Journal of Pediatrics*, 157, S60–S66; Lia, D., Pickell, L., Liu, Y., Wu, Q., Cohn, J. S., and Rozen, R. (2005). Maternal methylenetetrahydrofolate reductase deficiency and low dietary folate lead to adverse reproductive outcomes and congenital heart defects in mice. *American Journal of Clinical Nutrition*, 82, 188–195.

241 Jarvenpaa, J., Pakkila, M., Savolainen, E. R., Perheentupa, A., Jarvela, I., and Ryynanen, M. (2006). Evaluation of Factor V Leiden, prothrombin and methylenetetrahydrofolate reductase gene in patients with severe pregnancy complications in northern Finland. *Gynecologic and Obstetric Investigation*, 62, 28–32.

242 National Society of Genetic Counselors. Retrieved from www.nsgc.org, on 9/25/2008.

243 Wren, K. (2004, October 21). "Systems biology" focuses on turning masses of genetic data into treatments for disease. Retrieved from www.msnbc.msn.com/id/6291903/, on 9/25/2008.

244 Condit, C. M., Dubriwny, T., Lynch, J., and Parrott, R. (2004). Lay people's understanding of and preference against the word "mutation." *American Journal of Medical Genetics*, 130A, 245–250.

245 Adamzik, M., Frey, U. H., Riemann, K., Sixt, S., Lehmann, N., Siffert, W., and Peters, J. (2008). Factor V Leiden mutation is associated with improved 30-day survival in patients with acute respiratory distress syndrome. *Critical Care Medicine*, 36, 177–179.

246 Kerlin, B. A., Yan, S. B., Isermann, B. H., Brandt, J. T., Sood, R., Basson, B. R., Joyce, D. E., Wiler, H., and Dhainaut, J. (2003). Survival advantage associated with heterozygous Factor V Leiden mutation in patients with severe sepsis and in mouse endotoxemia. *Blood*, 102, 3085–3092.

247 Human Genome Project information: Pharmacogenomics. Retrieved from www.ornl.gov/sci/techresources/Human_Genome/medicine/pharma.shtml, on 9/26/2008.

248 Coumadin. Retrieved from www.rxlist.com/coumadin-drug/article.htm, on 9/25/2008.

249 Heck, A. M., DeWitt, B. A., and Lukes, A. (2000). Potential interactions between alternative therapies and warfarin. *American Journal of Health-Systems Pharmacy*, 57, 1221–1230.

250 PT and INR. Retrieved from http://labtestsonline.org/understanding/analytes/pt/test.html, on 9/25/2008.

251 Rettie, A. N. (2008). Pharmacogenomics of 4-hydroxycoumarin anti-coagulants. *Drug Metabolic Review*, 40, 355–375.

252 Yaktine, A. L., and Pool, R. (2007). *Nutrigenomics and Beyond: Informing the future – Workshop summary*. Institute of Medicine Report. Washington, DC: National Academies Press.

253 Goldman, D., Oroszi, G., and Ducci, F. (2005). The genetics of addictions: Uncovering the genes. *Focus*, 4, 401–415.

254 Lerman, C., Shields, P. G., Wileyto, E. P., Audrain, J., Pinto, A., Hawk, L., Krishnan, S., and Epstein, L. (2002). Pharmacogenetic investigation of smoking cessation treatment. *Pharmacogenetics*, 12, 627–634.

255 Murff, H., Byrne, D., and Syngal, S. (2004). Cancer risk assessment: Quality and impact of the family history interview. *American Journal of Preventive Medicine, 27,* 239–245.

256 Goldstein, A. M., Stacey, S. N., Olafsson, J. H., Jonsson, G. F., Helgason, A., Sulem, P., Sigurgeirsson, B., Benediktsdottir, K. R., Thorisdottir, K., Ragnarsson, R., Kjartansson, J., Kostic, J., Masson, G., Kristjansson, K., Gulcher, J. R., Kong, A., Thorsteinsdottir, U., Rafnar, T., Tucker, M. A., and Stefansson, K. (2008). CDKN2A mutations and melanoma risk in the Icelandic population. *Journal of Medical Genetics, 45,* 284–285.

257 Finkler, K. (2000). *Experiencing the New Genetics: Family and kinship on the medical frontier.* Philadelphia, PA: University of Pennsylvania Press.

258 Juengst, E. T., Genetic testing and the moral dynamics of family life. *Public Understanding of Science, 8,* 193–205.

259 Korobkin, R., and Rajkumar, R. (2008). The Genetic Information Nondiscrimination Act – a half-step toward risk sharing. *New England Journal of Medicine, 359,* 335–337.

260 Pontious, J. M. (2002, January). Understanding the "worried well" – commentary. *Journal of Family Practice, 51,* 30.

261 Henderson, L., and Kitzinger, J. (1999). The human drama of genes: "hard" and "soft" representations of breast cancer genetics. *Sociology of Health and Illness, 21,* 560–578.

262 Hoskins et al. (1995). See 174 above.

263 Duncan, V. J., Parrott, R. L., and Silk, K. J. (2001). African American women's perceptions of the role of genetics in breast cancer risk. *American Journal of Health Studies, 17,* 50–58.

264 Andrykowski, M. A., Munn, R. K., and Studts, J. L. (1996). Interest in learning of personal genetic risk for cancer: A general population survey. *Preventive Medicine, 25,* 527–536.

265 SYNGENE. Retrieved from www.syngene.com, on 9/25/2008.

266 Identity theft – A primer. Retrieved from www.privcom.gc.ca/id/primer_e.asp, on 8/2/2008; More about identity theft: What is it? Facts and figures. Retrieved from www.europ-assistance.co.uk/Template.aspx?ID=229, on 8/2/2008.

267 Schoen, C., Osborn, R., Huynh, P. T., Doty, M., Peugh, J., and Zapert, K. (2006). On the front lines of care: Primary care doctors' office systems, experiences, and views in seven countries. *Health Affairs, 25,* 555–571.

268 The medical identity theft information page. Retrieved from www.worldprivacyforum.org/medicalidentitytheft.html, on 9/25/2008.

269 MIB (formerly the Medical Information Bureau). Retrieved from http://survivorshipatoz.org/sub/php?aid=987, on 7/22/2008; MIB Privacy policy. Retrieved from www.mib.com/html/mib_privacy_policy.html, on 4/15/2008; Your medical records: Make sure your medical profile

is a healthy, accurate description of you. Retrieved from http://searchenginez.com/medical_records_usa.html, on 7/22/2008.

270 Medids.com Medical card generation form. Retrieved from www.medids.com/phorm/phorm.php, on 9/26/2008.

271 Struewing, J. P., Hartge, P., Wacholder, S., Baker, S. M., Berlin, M., McAdams, M., Timmerman, M. M., Brody, L. C., and Tucker, M. A. (1997). The risk of cancer associated with specific mutations of BRCA1 and BRCA2 among Ashkenazi Jews. *New England Journal of Medicine*, 336, 1401–1408.

272 National biospecimen network, Retrieved from http://biospecimens.cancer.gov/biospecimen/network/, on 9/25/2008.

273 Secretary's Advisory Committee on Genetics, Health, and Society (2007). Policy issues associated with undertaking a new large US population cohort study of genes, environment, and disease. Retrieved from www4.od.nih.gov/oba/sacghs/reports/SACGHS_LPS_report.pdf, on 12/19/2007.

Index